"Myrica meets eac

the fullness of Love, laughter, and respect. she shares within the pages of this beautiful book is coming from a deep place of reverence for the tradition of Ayurveda. Each page is brimming with valuable information, delicious recipes, and practical cleansing techniques. Her own life is a radiant example of how, when the healing principles of Ayurveda are applied consistently, radical healing and miracles result. Myrica continues to be an inspiration to me and so many others."

– Sarah Kruse
Ayurvedic Practitioner, LMP

"Myrica Morningstar is one of the most radiant beings on the planet. She was my first Ayurvedic massage teacher, whom I had the privilege to meet back in 1997. She was already guiding people through panchakarma even at that time. She has not stopped since. This has been her life's work. It's what she does. Who she IS. She lives the life and detox secrets that she shares humbly with us here. A rare teacher who guides from her heart, Myrica has blessed us with her long-awaited debut book. In it she distills the essence of her lifetime of healing wisdom, personal evolution, and detoxification methods and recipes for easy transformation of all aspects of one's life - well beyond that of the body. Thank you, Myrica, for your beautiful offering, lifetime of love, and friendship."

– Traci Webb
Northwest Institute of Ayurveda

Healing & Transformation Through

The Art & Practice of Panchakarma

Seasonal Cleansing in the Ayurvedic Tradition

By Myrica Morningstar

SHAKTI MA PUBLISHING

Dedication

I DEDICATE THIS BOOK TO YOU, beloved reader.
May your inner being be deeply nourished
so that all that is beautiful and all that is golden
illuminates your mind, shines from your heart,
and gives you the strength to move
through life in grace & joy.

The Art & Practice of Panchakarma

To inform and empower you to create within your body and mind an optimum environment for healing to take place and to maximize your body's ability to heal itself through using the principles of Ayurveda and seasonal cleansing is the goal of this book.

This information is not intended for use in the diagnosis, treatment, or cure of any disease. If you have any serious acute or chronic health concern, please consult a trained health professional who can fully assess your needs and address them effectively. Check with your doctor before taking herbs or using essential oils when pregnant or nursing.

Healing & Transformation Through
The Art & Practice of Panchakarma
Seasonal Cleansing in the Ayurvedic Tradition

First Edition
Shakti Ma Publishing

Published 2018 by Shakti Ma Publishing

Cover Art:
Shara Gardner

Book Design and Illustrations pp. 120-124:
Diane Rigoli, RigoliCreative.com

Illustration p. 83: Lily Maxfield

Editing:
Mar Goodman
David Rhodes
Sarah Kruse
Traci Webb
Jenna Graven

ISBN: 978-0-692-93794-5
Printed in U.S.A.

Table of Contents

"*We are capable of recreating our lives continually at deeper and higher levels of freedom, beauty, and bliss. We are limited only by our beliefs about what is possible and what we deserve according to our definition of "self."*

– Myrica Morningstar

INTRODUCTION

Taking Full Response-Ability for Your Life

We are a part of all that is, intimately connected to everything through the web of life.

Arising from One Source, we are so much more magnificent than we have been taught to believe. Life is an intricately woven holographic fabric from which all beings and all things arise, each in a unique vibrational pattern. We are a golden thread of sound and light in the constantly woven tapestry of life. And ... we are also the weavers!

We are capable of recreating our lives continually at deeper and higher levels of freedom, beauty, and bliss. We are limited only by our beliefs about what is possible and what we deserve according to our definition of "self."

We are living in the midst of a period of rebalancing at a scale which we have not seen before in our recorded history. This is a time of a great reorganization at every level of experience, from the personal to the planetary. All of life is experiencing the stress of polarization, and many are struggling to cope with or adapt to the current state of our physical, emotional, and social environments. It is vital that we cultivate strength, calm, and clarity that will allow us to respond creatively and compassionately to life's circumstances and bring benefit to all.

We cannot wait for someone else to find solutions to the many challenges that face us today. We must find the ways and start living them. Any efforts made, anything accomplished or modeled by anyone will open the way for others to find their own unique purpose and gifts.

The seasonal cleansing practices outlined in this book show ways to bring more balance and harmony to your body, mind, and emotions; therefore, to all of life. Create an intentional time to turn your focus inward. Become quiet. Feel your body, listen to your heart, and become aware of your thoughts. This will allow you to start to become a compassionate witness to your habitual patterns. You will discover that the thoughts and feelings that arise are yours, but they are not YOU. Your body is a gift through which you experience life in this dimension. From the vantage point of this expanded awareness, you have a chance to choose more empowering and loving thoughts and actions towards yourself and others.

Implementing these practices may increase your well-being, boost your immunity and adaptability. You may find yourself energized, clear, and more capable to meet life in the best possible way. You may also increase your ability to receive guidance, inspiration, and creative solutions from your innermost being. Your sense of well-being will radiate to others as it ripples out from you into the field we all experience. The benefits of this practice extend far beyond your self. This is a profound gift for everyone in your life: your spouse, children, grandchildren, friends, community, and ultimately the world.

When we cherish this life, sharing love and thanks generously, caring for our self and all within our sphere of influence, life magically transforms into a field of beauty and possibility! Our life is a direct reflection of our consciousness.

This book shows a way to regularly release the toxicity of unprocessed thoughts, feelings, emotions, and sensory input, as well as environmental toxins. The release of these toxic patterns allows your natural state of relaxed vibrancy to express once again, which is vital to anchor the new human. Toward this aspiration, I make this humble offering.

I recommend that you read this book all the way through at least once before trying to implement the practices which it describes. Perhaps read it once through, highlighting or bookmarking the practices that seem like they will most effectively help you. If you are new to the system of Ayurveda, as you read about the qualities of the elements and how they manifest, start to identify which of those qualities best describes you.

You will benefit most by working with a skilled Ayurvedic practitioner who can determine your constitution, your current state, and help you outline a treatment protocol specific to your needs. This book is a lovely companion and guide to take you deeper into the process of approaching panchakarma as a sacred ritual.

May this book bring benefit to you and yours. Through the actual experience of these practices, you will transform the philosophy of Ayurveda and yoga into a living, breathing wisdom that comes from practice and eventually a deep knowing.

Please know that everything contained in these pages is a reflection of my own experience. I am not a medical doctor and I do not diagnose or treat disease. This information is not in any way meant to replace any medical care you may need. All information on herbs or healing procedures introduced here is based on ancient practices of Ayurveda and yoga. You are encouraged to do your own research before engaging in these practices.

CHAPTER ONE

Turning, Turning Toward Life – My Healing Story

On May 13th, 1988, a Friday (Friday the 13th is historically a lucky day for me), I lay in my cozy bed, sound asleep with my precious five week old daughter, Lily Grace, in my arms, the river outside our home singing her springtime melody.

I was awakened suddenly with the most excruciating pain I can remember ever experiencing. It was way beyond childbirth. The pain moved from the inside of my head and out my left ear. It lasted only seconds, maybe a minute. But when it was over, my husband asked me in a panic if I wanted to go to the clinic. "No, I'm fine now." When it happened again in about 15 minutes, I surrendered. "OK, we'd better go." We left our other three children with our trusted friends and neighbors who lived in a cabin just across the yard.

I remember it all so clearly: sitting on the end of the examination table, our beloved local country doc running a pin across my face to see if I had any feeling there. Hmmm ... none on one side. No gag reflex on that side either. He sent us to the hospital, an hour away, for a CT scan. I remember the disbelief, shock, and numbness I felt, my infant in my arms, as they showed me the x-ray image of a brain tumor. Next thing I remember was sitting in a neurosurgeon's office, a well-meaning man was saying that I needed to have brain surgery to remove the tumor. The good news was that it was most likely benign and slow growing, a real blessing to me since that meant I had some time to consider my options.

An image came to me of my uncle Cal. He had brain surgery and was never quite the same afterwards. I had 4 kids and a beautiful life ahead of me! I just didn't want to go there. So, I asked about alternatives. He informed me that I could have chemotherapy and radiation instead of the surgery, but he wouldn't recommend it. I asked him, "What would happen if I didn't have it removed?" It was already occurring to me that I might be able to shrink this thing myself. He told me, "You would be dead within 15 years." Inside I was saying to myself, "Cancel Cancel Cancel." I left his office in a daze, not knowing what I would do, but knowing I was not ready to undergo brain surgery. At least not then! If I ever got clear guidance to have the surgery, I could always do it later. But I wasn't ready for that yet.

Lily and I climbed into our car and I looked at my husband. The first words out of his mouth were, "You know, the body isn't real." (He was studying *The Course in Miracles* at the time.) At this point, 29 years later, with all I know now, I can relate to his statement a whole lot more than I could when I was a young mother of 4 children with a diagnosis of a brain tumor. I remember thinking, "OK, I'm on my own here." On one end of the spectrum, the neurosurgeon was saying I needed to have brain surgery in order to survive, and on the other end, my partner was saying I didn't need to do anything. I knew I needed to do SOMETHING, but I had no idea what! There was a long silence, and then I heard myself say, "Let's go get a wheat grass juice at the co-op." With that statement, I took the first step on my healing journey.

Following inner guidance, I bought a book by Bernard Jensen on colon cleansing. I got all of the things he recommended for a cleanse: bentonite clay, niacin tablets, pancreatic enzymes (having been vegetarian for 18 years, I struggled a bit because they were made from a bovine source) and an array of vegetables for juicing. Intuitively I knew I wanted to start with this cleanse no matter what else I did. Fasting and colon cleansing were not new to me. I had done fasts in my twenties and had spent many hours poring over *Back to Eden* by Jethro Kloss, a comprehensive book on herbs and natural healing methods. Kloss extolled the miraculous benefits of colon cleansing for clearing up all manner of afflictions.

Over the next few days, I immersed myself in the colon cleansing book and created a protocol for myself of all of the different times of day I needed to take supplements or do something else, and I chose to go on a strict raw foods diet. I ate very little, if any, fruit. Summer was coming on and it was easy to make fresh juices and lots of salads. I had a garden started and planted more, so vegetables were plentiful. My goal was to alkalize my system.

Shortly after the diagnosis, I went over to the next valley to have a consultation with a well-known herbalist to learn about formulas I could take to support my healing. He guided me toward three tinctures. One was the Hoxsey formula (although he didn't call it that), which is a cancer formula. I remember being somewhat alarmed by this, because no one had used the "C" word, yet! The next was red clover blossom for cleansing the blood, and the third was gingko, for increasing circulation to the brain. He also affirmed my choice of diet with a few additional suggestions. Off I went, feeling a bit more confident.

My friend, River, made me a colema board to further help with cleansing. A colema is a cross between an enema and a colonic, where you run a few gallons of water through your colon daily to remove the toxicity and "mucoid plaque" that are being released from your colon. I had very little come out, but some toxins and "mucoid plaque" were released, and I was excited about that.

At the time, we lived on the banks of a beautiful river in Southern Oregon. I spent many hours swimming, meditating and lying on the rocks, watching my children play, and enjoying the simple miracle of everyday life. I was so full of gratitude for each day, each moment I had with them! I was very engaged in celebrating the beauty of life, love, and nature. I became aware of my need to turn my attention toward taking care of myself, realizing that I had been living pretty much in service to my husband, children, and friends. It was now essential for me to reclaim my own energy and center.

I spent time absorbed in my healing books. I had many on my own shelves and borrowed and bought others to support my path. There was one story in Richard Moss's book *The Black Butterfly* that touched me profoundly. It was about a woman who had a grapefruit-sized tumor in her belly. She went into an ecstatic state (while dancing, if I remember correctly), and the tumor dissolved completely, overnight. This story set me on a path to discover others who had experienced spontaneous remissions. I bought a big book that was packed full of these accounts. The stories were very uplifting to read and truly enlightening because what I found was that spontaneous remissions happen in all sorts of different ways. So, my question became: what is the common thread in these various accounts?

I came to the understanding that the common thread was a confluence of elements absolutely unique to each person. Some of these were:

- Belief or faith in a higher power, a particular healer, or a healing modality
- A change in diet (lots of different ideas about this)
- A heightened awareness of feelings, emotional processing, or allowing emotions to arise and be felt, accepted, and released
- Radical truth telling. By "coming out of the closet" or "airing dirty laundry," energy and circumstances can shift profoundly
- Living your own dreams and passions rather than the wishes of someone else or what you've learned from the culture you are "supposed to" do or "have to" do

- Forgiveness
- Letting go of control, surrendering, allowing what is
- Changing habitual patterns of thinking and behaving that diminish the quality of your life in any way
- True intimacy, authenticity, and integrity (integrated inner experience with outward expression)
- Gratitude and appreciation, this perhaps more than anything else. When we give thanks and praise for all that we have and for the miracle of life, we amplify the good and send waves of healing messages through the mind and floods of healing chemicals throughout the body

A diagnosis creates a "pattern interrupt," which can spur an in-depth inner inquiry as to how you're living. I think of it as a message from the body to pause for reflection and look for the ways you could adjust your ways of living that would communicate a true commitment to be here and to make a contribution to life. This could look like no longer putting off things that you really want to do or re-prioritizing. Sometimes commitment is all it takes. I was committed to doing whatever it would take to save my life, even if it became obvious that I needed to have the surgery at another time.

During this time, I also learned about the placebo and the nocebo effects. Placebo and nocebo refer to positive and negative outcomes based on one's expectations about a treatment protocol they undertake. This was actually a bit disconcerting for me. You mean there wasn't any SURE WAY to heal? My own thoughts and feelings could make the difference in anything I did to heal myself? Yikes. Suddenly I felt very alone with my inner being. The quest became WHAT DO I BELIEVE IN? What do I think is going to be "The Way" FOR ME to bring about a spontaneous dissolving of this tumor? I did my best not to claim the tumor as "mine." It was a diagnosis, it was an x-ray, it was a catalyst. It was even a gift. But those were the only ways I made it "real" in my experience. In a very imminent way, I realized that if I didn't discover what I believed was my own path to healing and learn to care for myself, I might not be around to see my children grow up.

At some point in the journey, I realized how much energy I was giving away to others who didn't really nourish me. I dropped several people right out of my life (actually, I don't even think they noticed!) and reclaimed some more of my own time and energy for the ones that mattered most; maybe for the first time in my life, that also included me. My inner being became the most important being in my life.

I asked my friends to see me well and happy for years to come, to imagine me holding my grandchildren. Those I was close to (who could relate to it) embraced me in prayer and visualization. Thank you, beloved friends!

I got really honest with what I was feeling. I started risking going beyond my comfort zone as well as potentially "hurting others" in order to authentically tell the truth of what I was feeling and thinking. This was a major breakthrough in my process. Sometimes I would cross that very uncomfortable threshold and say how I felt about something that I heard someone say and discover that I had been mistaken. I had heard them incorrectly or misunderstood their intention.

.... Oh! .... Oops! ....

I came to see how I was filtering what others were saying through my own negative self-image. It was humbling and at the same time profoundly liberating! I was breaking out of my own self-imposed cage. I was allowing myself to be vulnerable and starting to experience the great gift of real intimacy. Into-me-see. Perhaps the greatest awakening of that time was witnessing my own ego nature and seeing what a fear-based perspective she had. Meanwhile I was identifying with a greater part of myself that could notice and learn to hold space for her, understand her, feel empathy towards her, and forgive her. This was the moment that redefined "me" and evoked great compassion for the human condition.

Another delightful player in my healing "chapter" was an energy healer named Marilyn. During our first conversation, she told me she was booked a year out but that she would see me. I went to see her once a week in a group and also once a week for a private session for some months. The first thing she said to me was, "Well, you've created a perfect back door out of here. Are you sure you want to stay?" I remember being struck by her genuine sincerity and non-judgment towards me. I'm sure I could have said "yes" or "no" and been met with the same kind of neutral support.

When I said yes, with Lily in my arms, she asked me to recall the times I had had thoughts of no longer wanting to be here. I told her that I had never had any suicidal thoughts, but then she asked me to look deeper. Look for those times when I was saying to myself that life was too hard, or I can't do this anymore. Or even more subtle messages to myself that I wouldn't mind an exit. Wow. I had to admit that I did have those kinds of thoughts! Doesn't everyone? Thus began our journey of raising my awareness of my inner story along with a sense of empowerment about how much I really could be creating my reality.

When observing me, she commented that I hadn't been living fully in my body, only from the heart up. She said my heart was very open and my mind was very active. I could relate to that, actually. I had never really been into sports or physical activities much, always feeling rather awkward and uncoordinated. So, we worked with the breath and riding the breath fully into and through the body. What I know now is that she was working with life force or "prana," "mana," "chi," or "ki," which is not really the breath, but rides on the breath and can be directed anywhere by the mind. She told me to go out and walk in the morning dew; to feel my feet on the earth and receive energy, strength, and support from the earth. Twenty years later there is quite a bit of information on this practice, called "Earthing."

She also encouraged me to wean my ten month old baby so that I wasn't losing energy out of my breasts. That was difficult for me, as it was my desire to nurse my babies for at least a year and closer to two years in order to give their immune systems as much strength as I could. Given the information that I was losing a lot of my own life force, I chose to wean Lily Grace with the intention of using as much life force as I could to heal myself.

During our sessions, Marilyn would yell at me "Breathe through your c**t!" And "breathe past your knees!" Then, one day she had her hands on my head. They were so hot they felt like they were almost burning my scalp! (She was a powerhouse! She told me once that she had blown out seven stereo systems in her healing room with "her" energy.) She was very engaged with me, instructing me to breathe into and through my feet. I was very focused and felt the energy moving. Next thing I knew she was yelling, "Push! Push! Push!" like I was giving birth or moving something very urgently. Suddenly, there was a large POP in the room. It was audible, but also a distinct and tangible energetic opening. She said, "Ok, that was it."

That was it? That was IT?! I was a bit stunned and questioning.What just happened? She informed me that I had just released the tumor from my energetic field and that it would take maybe 6 months for the physical to catch up because the physical dimension is more dense, vibrating at a lower frequency. Could it really be that simple? She suggested that I could get another MRI in about 6 months to confirm that it was gone and sent me home with instructions to be in silence and alone for 4 days to integrate what had just happened.

OK, so here I was, a mother of 4 children, including a baby. How was I going to manage being alone and in silence for 4 days? I did my best. I spent a lot of time alone. I did a lot of journaling.

I wasn't fully convinced that was it, even though I wanted to believe it. After quite a bit of processing, I found myself writing to my children, saying things I wanted to share with them as if I wasn't going to be here to share them when they were old enough to hear.

I caught myself.

In that moment, my children were in the house. I was outside writing to them. What was I doing with that precious moment? I could be with them NOW. I could love them NOW. And every now moment that comes. I turned in that moment toward life. In that grace is how I live to this day, all these years later! I am immensely grateful for life and all of the opportunities that arise to share love, laughter, tears, touch, taste, and breath.

When I next saw Marilyn, I confessed I was grappling with some doubt. She assured me that I could have the tumor back anytime I wanted it ... affirming the power of my thoughts and feelings once again. I noticed over the next couple of weeks that the back of my head, over my occipital area, broke out in many small pustules. I considered this the release of the energy that was previously identified as a tumor.

So, what was it that brought about a healing? Was it the energy work? The emotional honesty? The herbs? The cleansing? The change in diet? Or was it what was underlying all of these choices: an inner commitment to do whatever it took.

I was turning. Turning within, turning toward my authenticity, turning toward what was really important, turning toward truly loving and honoring myself and others. I was turning toward nature, toward life, listening to the silent messages of the river, the trees and plants, my children, all of it. I was opening up to all of the subtle messages from the universe, looking for guidance. I was seeing how everything affects everything else, dissolving the conditioned illusion of separation.

I started living more fully in the moment, making each moment count, not putting things off, because this just may be the last moment I have. Death became a beautiful messenger, showing me the preciousness of life. These realizations have informed my life and continue to color everything to this day. Most all of us are living in faith that life will continue, when really, life could end at any moment for any of us.

I have come to honor every being and every moment as precious. Every flower, every sunrise, every unique scent, all of the beautiful bird songs – all of it. Every relationship, all the love shared, every emotion felt, even the heartbreaks and disappointments are the evidence that I AM ALIVE! I am able to experience a full spectrum of feelings. I celebrate as much as I remember to. I praise and uplift as much as I can. I live in absolute awe at the consciousness that manifests as this diverse reality, and I am that.

This was the healing for me: the gift of living fully in each moment – right here, right now. The gift of the journey. I never had another MRI or CT scan. I've never had another experience that led me to believe that I needed to. Instead, I take each day that is given. I aspire to living fully in love, harmony, and beauty; with joy, gratitude, and Glory!

I have continued to follow the ways to live which honor the gift of life. One of the most beneficial practices that I not only keep, but study, expand, practice, and share is seasonal cleansing. I practice a method that pulls from more than one tradition but still has its roots in what has been called the "Mother of all healing arts," Ayurveda, which literally translates to "the knowledge of life." The art and practice of Ayurveda is one of raising awareness about who you are, where you're living, and what you need in order to live in harmony – physically, mentally, emotionally, spiritually, and environmentally. We are each unique. We each have our own path. By its very nature, Ayurveda is inclusive of all methods that support wholeness and wellness. I humbly offer this "method" and sincerely pray that it will support and enhance your life.

CHAPTER TWO

The Importance of Cyclical Cleansing

> *"Disease starts out humbly in the body, as some imperceptible imbalance, and proceeds from there. The outcome of a full-blown disease may be devastating, but it has been built up through insignificant everyday actions. What we eat and drink, how we behave, how our emotions affect us—these are small things. When they support well-being, we don't give them a second thought. But no action is lost on the body. We are always building. Every bite of food, every breath, every thought is like laying a brick, even if we aren't aware that we are building."*
>
> – Deepak Chopra

Raising awareness is a day by day or even a moment by moment practice. However, taking time twice a year to pause, reflect, and cleanse the body and mind creates a space to remember who you are and what you really want to do with your life. Taking this time may also help you avert a disease scenario that may be starting to form. The body is self-healing GIVEN THE OPTIMUM CONDITIONS that support re-balancing. This is easily demonstrated when our skin gets cut. If we keep it clean and protected from further damage, a cut will heal on its own. (I see this as nothing short of a miracle!)

If you can recognize the subtle signs of imbalance early enough, then you have a chance to choreograph more conducive conditions to allow a natural state of balance to manifest.

Many people are living largely in a state of disconnection from their true nature and from the natural world. Every day we are literally barraged with information as well as sensory and energetic input. There are great and pressing demands on our time, resources, and attention. We experience many forms of stress on a daily basis, environmental stress as well as self-generated stress.

Notice how often you are in a state of resistance to what is. Resistance is tension, and chronic tension leads to exhaustion. When you are exhausted, your natural immune function becomes depleted, and you are much more susceptible to influences from your environment.

Sadly, our environment – the air, water, and soil – is contaminated with toxic pollution from many sources. The majority of the "food" that is available in conventional grocery stores is grown on soil that is depleted of minerals, heavily processed, and/or genetically modified. Even if you are eating organically grown food, the toxicity in the environment is inescapable.

Our bodies have to process a whole array of substances that we, as biological beings of the natural world, don't know how to process and that do not support life. In the air we breathe, there are chemicals and metals from vehicles, industry, and jets. Toxic chemicals off-gas from everything that is manufactured from plastic, vinyl, or any synthetic materials. The mainstream food supply is tainted with pesticides, herbicides, preservatives, and hormones. There are the toxic substances that many people willingly ingest: alcohol, cigarettes, sugar, and pharmaceutical and recreational drugs. Then there are the invisible influences: radioactive particles, electro-magnetic frequencies, and an array of living organisms in the form of bacteria, viruses, molds, and fungi.

I do not say this to invoke fear in you but to help raise awareness for those who don't realize that this is what is happening and to offer ways to protect and care for yourself until we can collectively integrate more healthy ways of living.

Perhaps the most constant form of subtle stress our bodies must process is habitual negative thinking and the emotional responses to it. To a large degree our bodies, minds, nervous systems, and hearts are overwhelmed and overloaded no matter who we are or where we live. Until we make intentional time to turn inward and actually watch our own thought processes, we may not even be aware of how many negative thoughts we have in a day.

It does not help to fixate on what is wrong. However, that does not mean that we can ignore it either. I believe that as long as we are embodied on this planet, we have a sacred responsibility to life itself, to remember how to live in harmony within the mandala of nature. Many ARE aware, and we ARE finding sustainable solutions which haven't yet reached all the way into the mainstream of society so that they are readily available to all. Until they are, we must find ways to regain or nurture our strength and motivation in order to actualize widespread change for the benefit of all.

We each live at the center of our own universe. We affect everything, and we are affected by everything. Life is a perfect feedback system. It is vital to become aware of the messages from your inner being, your body, and your life.

The input you take in from the manifest world through your senses literally informs the energetic material that composes your body and steers your thoughts and emotions. What are the influences that are shaping you? Do you watch television? How much media input are you receiving? What kinds of messages do these sources promote? Much of what is being incessantly broadcast are subtle messages, either that we're not good enough (we need this car, that shampoo, or some kind of medication to be ok) or that the world is full of "threats" and we should be afraid and alarmed.

When we are in a state of equanimity, knowing ourselves, thinking clearly, and freely expressing our emotions, we are able to much more effectively process all that we take in through the senses. We can witness and discern what is true and beneficial. We can moderate which influences we want to be taking in.

You have a lot of choice in how to nourish yourself once you are awake to the great merit of doing so. This moment is the point of power. No matter what arises, in most cases you have the power to choose how you will respond to a situation that is happening NOW.

Taking time, even twice a year for a number of days, to make self-care the most important thing you're doing is a potent way to promote excellent health and well-being. Cleansing your physical and subtle bodies and finding stillness inside, to reflect, process, forgive, and let go is the most effective and powerful way I know to maintain excellent health and well-being as well as prevent disease from ever having a chance to manifest.

When you take the time to clear your mind and bodily tissues, you make yourself much more available to receive a more refined quality of inspiration and nourishment from your environment. This allows you to take your life to the next level, whatever that means for you.

CHAPTER THREE

The Gift of Ayurveda

In 1970, I lived in the South San Francisco Bay area, what is now widely known as Silicon Valley. The "Summer of Love" had happened, and living near Stanford University, I had the opportunity to attend various large music events. I was very much influenced by the emerging "alternative" culture that was questioning everything that our parents had taught us: religion, racism, war, women's roles, body image, style, music, relationships, diet; basically, all aspects of how we were "supposed to" live, think, and behave. I was definitely exploring the outside of the box as well as the inner realms of consciousness. My generation was coming of age at a major transitional point in social-cultural awakening. We were the living change!

It was also at this point that many, myself included, were captivated by the "back to the land" movement. I was reading *The Mother Earth News* and *Organic Gardening* magazines, which sat on my bookshelf next to *Be Here Now* and *The Prophet*, books that inspired so many of us towards a completely different way of thinking. We were moving out of suburbia and into the country, planting gardens, and teaching ourselves how to live a more healthy and holistic lifestyle.

It was an exciting time. It was our generation that really ushered in the natural foods movement and then the organic foods movement and the alternative healing movement. Of course, we were not the first, nor the pioneers in these movements, but because we were reaching for new and better ways to live, we found and adopted these natural pathways. We made them our own and integrated them into mainstream culture.

At the age of sixteen, I was introduced to the path of yoga. "Lilias, Yoga, and You" was a television show that changed my life! It was through her teachings and modeling of natural beauty and gentle manner that I was first inspired to adopt the practices of yoga. I started meditating, doing asana practice, and adopted a vegetarian diet.

My decision to become vegetarian happened in an instant when I saw baby calves being shot in the head on the TV news in order to drive the price of beef up! I was horrified and vowed in that moment not to have anything to do with that! And so, I started eating steamed potatoes and carrots ... every day ... I didn't know what to eat! I hadn't really eaten that many vegetables growing up. My childhood diet was largely boxed, canned, and frozen foods--cereal, bread, and sweets.

As soon as I was motivated to explore vegetarian cooking, I found my way to the local health food store in nearby Berkeley. One of the first books that I picked up was *Ten Talents, a Seventh Day Adventist* (egg-less, dairy-less) vegetarian cookbook that existed long before "vegan" was a household word.

This era was the beginning of what has become a lifelong quest to discover and at times invent my most optimal ways of living. This was the beginning of an era in which one component of the exploration was diet. I have experimented with all kinds of vegetarian diets: macrobiotic, fruitarian, yogic, vegan, and raw foods. Over the years I've gone through periods of eliminating different things from my diet: dairy products, fats and oils, eggs, sugars, and wheat. I learned through my own experiences with these different experiments. I was always reaching for the answer to the question, "what is THE BEST diet?" The problem was that my perceptions about what was "best" kept changing. It was one thing when I was a teenager, then it changed when I got pregnant, was different when I was nursing a baby, and different again when I was in periods of hard physical work as opposed to periods of more artistic expression or caring for the needs of a family.

When I discovered the path of Ayurveda in 1994, I found an answer to that question that I had been exploring for so many years: There is no "best" diet for everyone all the time. Each of us is unique. We have different needs at different times of life. We have different inherited cultural influences.

In 1994, when I was 39 years old, I reached a major transition point in my own journey. Finding myself alone with 4 children to raise, I asked for guidance and direction while in meditation. In one of the few times I have actually received an audible message from Spirit, I heard the phrase, "Consultations in joyful living." Hmmmmm ... What exactly did that mean?

I sought the guidance of a beloved wise woman counselor since my life was in a state of turmoil and change. When I told her about my message from God, she encouraged me to go home and make up a brochure. That was a really great assignment, because it helped me to think about what gifts I had to offer others on the subject of joyful living.

Another serendipitous event occurred right after receiving this assignment, when I went to a bookstore on my way home. Do you know how a book will sometimes almost jump off a shelf at you? That happened to me that day with a book titled *A Woman's Best Medicine, Health, Happiness, and Long Life through Ayurveda* by Nancy Lonsdorf, Veronica Butler, and Melanie Brown. Opening the book I read, "Ayurveda is the path of living joyfully." Aha! I bought the book and took it home. I was so moved by things I was reading that I would call my dear friend and read segments to her over the phone. That book initiated a journey for me that has helped me, my family, and my communities in countless ways. I am so grateful.

My journey on the path of Ayurveda expanded me beyond my concepts and ideas about food and health (and every other aspect of life) into experiencing a much greater context for knowing who I am and living in harmony with all of life.

The cleansing practices I am introducing in this book come from the practice of panchakarma, Ayurveda's most profound cleansing, re-balancing, and rejuvenating practice.

Ayurveda is practiced as a medical science; however, the most profound and basic principle of Ayurveda is in teaching us how to live a balanced life, in harmony with nature, through daily lifestyle practices. Ayurveda belongs in every home. It has immense value to inform life's most foundational practices: what we eat, how we eat, simple herbal supports, and daily and seasonal rituals that promote and maintain physical health, mental health, and emotional stability.

Ayurveda is a subject that is as vast and diverse as life itself. The study and practice of Ayurveda over these 20 plus years has contributed to my good health and more — to my ever-expanding awareness, deep love, and exuberant joy.

In the next chapters, I offer you an introduction and my own interpretation of Ayurveda and then invite you to have your own experience with this profound practice.

Ayurveda is a system that is based in nature. In many ways it is very simple, and yet it is so deep, complex, intricate, and individual that you could study Ayurveda for the rest of your life and never reach a full understanding of it. It is like life itself; you can aspire to understand and experience it in the best way you can from your own unique perspective, and yet there is infinitely more to it than can be experienced or known. My aspiration is to embody Ayurveda, that I may experience life in radiant health and balance, living in grace without distraction from dis-ease.

The true gift of Ayurveda is the context that it provides for understanding life and ourselves. Ayurveda (and yogic philosophy) describes us as pure spirit, ether, manifesting in different vibrational frequencies: air, fire, water, and earth; thought, emotion, and body.

When you notice that you can see and touch your body, you can watch thoughts coming and going, you can experience emotions moving through your field, perhaps you can start to identify yourself as the one (presence) who can witness yourself in a variety of circumstances. With attention, you will be able to start discerning patterns of thought and action that are life promoting from those that are not, IF YOU ARE AWAKE AND AWARE OF YOURSELF. That's a big IF.

One of the most fundamentally profound practices you can develop is the capacity to identify with and observe yourself from the perspective of the neutral witness. As you become the observer of your body, mind, and emotional natures, you step into an expanded state of awareness, which is a much more empowered position. As the observer, you are no longer solely identified as your body, your pain, your thoughts, your emotions, or your patterns of behavior. They are yours, but they are not YOU.

So often we adopt habitual ways of perceiving, thinking about, and responding to the circumstances that life presents that we lose sight of the full range of possible ways to look at things. We forget to think in more expansive and creative ways or to respond to situations in fresh ways.

Perhaps your parents were very serious in their approach to life. In that case, it's very likely that you would adopt an unconscious, serious view of life as well, losing sight of the ability to laugh at life or to have a fun, light attitude. Or perhaps the people around you taught you to perceive and evaluate life through your intellect rather than your heart, in which case you may have a tendency to overthink things or lack a deeply compassionate heart. If you can become a witness to these kinds of patterns in yourself, whatever they may be, then suddenly you have expanded your view as well as your options!

Once you have the opportunity to discover what you are NOT, then you are free to explore the realms of what you ARE.

What you are, at the core of your being, is pure consciousness. When you discover this and you develop the ability to witness yourself, you can ascend to the position of director of your life. As you watch the play, you can choose to make adjustments to the script, the players, or the scenery to bring about the essence of what you want to express and experience through your life. You are no longer a victim of life's circumstances but realize you have creative choices in how you think, feel, and respond.

What I am pointing to here is a path of self-discovery, in which the healing of the self (the individual self-image) leads to self-mastery (integrity with the soul nature.) In nature, there is always wholeness. Your life is a perfect feedback system.

So again, the key is awareness. As you move through your day, check in and ask yourself, "How do I feel about this?" or "What is running me right now?" Increase your awareness about your choices and responses to life. As you look at your choices, thoughts, and emotional responses to food, news, possessions, relationships, your work, sleep patterns ... anything ... ask yourself, "Is this an automatic response? Is this my habitual reaction to this situation, or am I responding consciously? Whose voice am I hearing right now? Am I being nourished by my choices and responses? Are they serving my life? Is this what I really want right now?"

Our bodies are thought-reactive. We are constantly recreating ourselves through our mental and emotional interpretation of the information we receive through the five senses. And we are continually manifesting our lives by the actions we take or don't take.

"*Man forms his future by his actions. His every good or bad action spreads its vibrations and becomes known throughout the universe. The more spiritual a man is, the stronger and clearer are the vibrations of his actions, which spread over the world and weave his future. The universe is like a dome: it vibrates to that which you say in it and echoes the same back to you. So also is the law of action: we reap what we sow.*"

– Hazrat Inayat Khan

CHAPTER FOUR

Know Thyself as Elemental Consciousness

I invite you on a journey that has the potential to change your life in many beneficial ways. Please be gentle with yourself and others that you share these practices with. Changing habitual patterns can be very challenging. Exercise compassion and learn to laugh at yourself and with others as you begin to wake up and see the energies that have been running you. Give thanks that you can see it happening, and persevere. This is the process of conscious evolution.

The practices you will learn here are inspired by my studies and practice of Ayurveda. Ayurveda is one of the most comprehensive health care systems in the world, addressing physical, mental, emotional, and spiritual health. The level of health I am referring to is not the mere absence of disease but radiant aliveness, inner peace, abundant energy, strength, commitment, clarity of purpose, and a true ability to manifest your essential nature.

The teachings of Ayurveda come from the Vedas, the ancient holy texts of India. Ayurveda is at least 5000 years old. It predated and directly influenced many healing sciences including

Chinese medicine, Tibetan medicine, Greek medicine (which was the root of allopathic medicine), and holistic medicine in general. It is the health science of the yogic tradition, supporting the union of the human self with the divine Self.

I deeply honor the vast roots of Ayurveda in Indian culture and tradition; I also feel it is imperative that we embrace the practices that Ayurveda offers in a manner that honors our own ancestral roots and the culture we find ourselves living in now. The wisdom of Ayurveda is timeless. In fact, many aspects of this philosophy that have been around for thousands of years are now being verified by quantum physics!

Everything you can see, experience, or imagine is composed of the five elements arising from pure consciousness. The elements are patterns of intelligence, vibrational patterns resonating at different frequencies from the most subtle to the most dense: ether, air, fire, water, and earth. I have found it extremely beneficial to view and understand the nature of the elements through the lens of Ayurveda, which teaches how the fundamental elements of nature manifest as physical attributes, ways of thinking, and emotional predilections. When the elements are expressing in accordance with your true essential nature, they allow all the natural functions of the body and mind to manifest perfect love, harmony, and beauty. Let me elaborate.

The Sanskrit word for optimal health is svastha, meaning "Established in Self." Being established in Self means having the ability to maintain the connection to your essential nature, grounding it in your experiences through the ever-changing conditions of life. When you are established in your Self, your body, mind, and heart are serving you in living your dharma, your purpose.

Dis-ease is any condition of the body or mind that results in anything less than the full expression of the highest nature of the individual: balanced energy, spontaneous joy, deep wisdom, and bliss in all of life. All dis-ease begins when we forget our essential nature. There is a Sanskrit word for this: prajnaparadha, meaning not listening to your inner intelligence; it's a lack of knowledge, an ignorance. An example of this is when you know you really shouldn't ____ (fill in the blank), but you do it anyway.

Here is the way that Ayurveda views the elements and how they manifest throughout life, not only through humans, but through all of nature. My first teacher suggested I start looking for the ways in which all of the elements express through nature. Once my eyes were opened, I was given a whole new context for viewing life.

ETHER

The element ether is called "Akasha" in Sanskrit. It is omnipresent, all pervading, silent space from which all things arise and exist. The Vedas describe ether as the source and existence of all matter. The qualities of ether are clear, light, cold, subtle, and immeasurable. It is described as such because of its lack of substance, heat, weight, etc.

In quantum physics, ether is referred to as "the vacuum" or "the field." Although in the West, we think of the space between things as empty, it's really full of endless potential. We each access this field directly. All life, including yours, lives in and from the field. I have learned that we can access this source field through our hearts in meditation. The silent depth of our being is always there, but we don't always tune into it because the mind is busy chattering away and the senses are receiving and processing information every moment. It is so immensely valuable to develop the ability to quiet the mind, the emotions, and the senses in order to access this silent space where all potentialities arise. This is the pure presence that simply is, the silent expansive backdrop to all experience, the throne of the EXPERIENCER, where resistance falls away and consciousness expands.

You live at the center of your own experience within the field. You directly interact with the field through the thoughts and the feelings that you generate. Just as you are susceptible to the collective thoughts and beliefs of others through the field, you also can directly affect the field with intentional thinking, prayer or focused intentions, behaviors, and actions. Everything is connected within a whole system. There is perfect feedback from the system in relation to what you, individually and collectively, put into it.

Everything in the manifest world arises from the field: ether.

AIR

Air or "vayu" is movement through space. An impulse of thought is a "sound," a fluctuation in vibration in the field. Audible sounds are a slightly more dense vibration. For example, a word has more substance than a thought. When we name something or speak anything, we give it more reality. It is essential to remember that thoughts and words activate all kinds of responses in your own being, in other beings, and in the entire field of space/time. Conscious thinking and speaking (even self-talk) is key in generating well-being and a truly great life.

The air element in your body is responsible for all movement: breath, heartbeat, thoughts, circulation of blood, lymph, peristalsis, elimination through the bowels and bladder, and nerve impulses.

Air is the prime force of the nervous system. It governs sensory and mental balance, your sensory and motor orientation, and gives you mental adaptability and comprehension. It is the basic vital life force (prana), deriving primarily from breath.

The qualities of air are light, dry, cold, and moving.

People who have more air influence are generally more visionary, intuitive, creative, telepathic, and enthusiastic. They tend to be more artistically oriented, more psychic, and generally less grounded people.

Physically, air types are often thin and light, either tall or short, have drier skin, small eyes, thin lips, dry curly hair, darker skin, and tend to get cold (or hot) more easily.

In the subtle realms, balanced air types are bubbly, enthusiastic, inspired, "spiritual," creative, and quick-minded. Out of balance air types could be overwhelmed, spacey, anxious, or fearful. Those who have a lot of air influence are more easily moved off of their center.

Physical symptoms of air imbalance are pain, weakness, excess gas, constipation, brittleness, dryness, roughness, emaciation, and nervous system disorders.

FIRE

Fire or "agni" is the next density of frequency. The energy of fire is the energy of transformation of all sensory input into your body/mind organism. Fire transforms food into energy and thoughts into actions and feelings. Emotion = e-motion = energy in motion. The fire energy in the heart is called passion. Fire is the light of the mind that discerns reality and inspires your passions. The fire energy is also the light shining from your eyes.

The fire element is manifest as the digestive fire (especially the functions of the small intestine and liver), the blood, and the endocrine system. It also gives color and luster to your skin.

People with more fire energy tend to be more athletic, medium frame, with a rosy or ruddy complexion, fine, straight hair, and intense, bright eyes.

Subtly, fire is very sharp and penetrating. People that have more fire energy are more intense, driven, passionate, detail-oriented, often perfectionists.

The qualities of fire are hot and sharp.

A balanced fire type will be warm, passionate, organized, clear-minded, sharp, bright, and goal-oriented.

Out of balance fire types can be perfectionists, quick to anger, jealous, critical, and judgmental. Physically an out of balance fire type might have inflammation, skin issues, liver issues, hyper-acidity, or high blood pressure.

WATER

Water or "jala" is the next density of vibration. It carries the energy of cooling, lubricating, softening, protecting, and allowing for flow. Water carries information throughout the system. The human body is 70% water.

Here's something to think about: In Masaru Emoto's work on water, he shows very clearly that the structure of water is instantly changed by thoughts, feelings, and emotions.

The quality of water is cool and soft.

People with more water in their constitution tend to sweat more easily. They have soft skin and thick luxurious hair.

When balanced, water-type people are gentle, loving, compassionate, and tender. They tend to be able to flow with things.

When out of balance, they can become overly attached or overly sentimental.

Physically, the main symptoms of imbalance are swelling, excess mucous, dampened digestive fire, and nausea.

EARTH

Earth or "prithvi" is the most dense frequency, the most "solid." The element of earth is hard, stable, still, strong, grounded, and slow.

Earth is cool and solid.

An earth-type person is heavier-boned, stocky, with a thick neck, short fingers and toes, large eyes, and full lips, hips, and breasts.

When balanced, they tend to be patient, loving, devoted, grounded, and dependable.

When out of balance, earth-types tend towards stubbornness, complacency, and lethargy. Physically, an imbalance in the earth element could show up as stagnation in the mind or body, excess sleeping, or excess tissue in the form of fat or tumors.

CHAPTER FIVE

Doshas and Subtle Doshas

In the science of Ayurveda, these elements combine together in specific ways to form what are known as the three doshas: vata, pitta, and kapha.

Understanding your predominant dosha basically helps you to understand the ways in which you tend to go out of balance and also helps you to understand the ways you can care for yourself in the most beneficial ways. Here is the briefest of descriptions:

Vata = Ether and Air

Space and movement. Ether is cold and light, air is dry and movable; so, vata is cold, light, dry, and moving. Vata is the catabolic force in nature and predominates at the end of life. People with a lot of vata qualities need to balance in ways that are warming, grounding, moist, and still. Consistency is very beneficial for balancing vata types.

Pitta = Fire and Water

Pitta is light, hot, oily, and moist and is the metabolic force which predominates at mid-life. People with a lot of pitta qualities need to balance in ways that are cooling, grounding, and drying. Chilling out more is balancing for pitta types.

Kapha = Water and Earth

Kapha is cold, heavy, and wet. Kapha is the anabolic force which predominates from conception to adolescence, when one is growing their body. People with a lot of kapha qualities need to balance in ways that are warm, light, and drying. Movement and stimulation are beneficial to balance kapha energy.

To further dazzle the mind, the doshas also combine together to make 10 different types. I am going to list them but encourage you to seek out further reading to learn more. This book has a different focus and intention. Banyan Botanicals has great descriptions of the different doshas and doshic combinations on their website, www.banyanbotanicals.com.

Vata
Pitta
Kapha
Vata-Pitta
Vata-Kapha
Pitta-Vata
Pitta-Kapha
Kapha-Vata
Kapha-Pitta
Vata-Pitta-Kapha

The most common are dual-types. There are fewer people that are tridoshic or have a single dosha.

Take some time to think about these qualities. What type or combination of types are you? We each have all of the elements in us, but we tend to have some qualities more predominantly than others.

Your constitution is called prakruti in Ayurveda. It is the balance of energies at the moment of conception, based on the balance of energies of each of your parents IN THAT MOMENT and your own soul's journey of evolution. Your prakruti doesn't change throughout your lifetime.

However, life is in a constant state of change. We are affected by every bit of sensory input, every thought, word, belief, experience, and feeling. Where you are right now is the culmination of every experience you have had since conception.

Vikruti is the name for what we see NOW, which is the accumulation of every experience you have had since that moment of conception. So, in utero, during birth, infancy, childhood, teenage, and adult years, each moment you have been receiving information through the senses that has brought you to who you are right now.

Sometimes it can be difficult to assess yourself. Seeking out a trusted practitioner can often help you to see yourself more clearly through the eyes of Ayurveda. When an Ayurvedic practitioner is working with you, we are striving to bring your vikruti into alignment with your prakruti. This is your unique expression of balance.

It is valuable to know yourself and to understand in what ways you have a tendency to go out of balance. This will help you in determining how to manage all aspects of your life so that you can be supported to be the best that you can be.

Identifying your dosha is really identifying your propensity to go out of balance. The doshas are not who you ARE. Who you are is LIFE FORCE INTELLIGENCE, LIGHT, and LOVE.

These three primary energies when balanced are called prana, tejas, and ojas and when imbalanced are called vata, pitta, and kapha.

> *"Who you are is LIFE FORCE, LIGHT, and LOVE focalized through a human organism."*
>
> – Jai Dev Singh

THE SUBTLE DOSHAS

You've learned a bit about vata, pitta, and kapha, the three doshas, as a way of describing how the five elements function as the energies that express through your body, mind, and emotions. Now, I would like to dive a little deeper into to the even more subtle energies that are said to precede the doshas: prana, tejas, and ojas.

Prana is the most subtle form of vata. Tejas is the subtle form of pitta, and ojas the most subtle form of kapha. When physical, mental, and spiritual "digestion" are optimal, these subtle doshas produce the elements as the dhatus (tissue layers) in perfect quanties to perform necessary bodily functions.

Prana ~ the most subtle form of vata dosha

The nature of prana is movement, and it is often associated with the breath. Prana is not the breath, yet it rides on the breath, entering and exiting your body following the movement of breath. You also take in prana by experience of touch and taking in food and water. Also, mind and prana are two aspects of the same phenomenon. Prana is the principle of movement, and mind is the principle of intelligence. Therefore, all actions require prana, including thinking. By slowing down your breath, your thoughts are slowed down. Try it right now! It's so easy to have a DIRECT experience of this valuable tool.

In Ayurveda it is said that all disease can be treated through the normalization of prana. Prana communicates to all areas of the body and mind. Wherever there is pain in the body, there is a lack of prana. Pain is the body's call for attention. Take the time to listen and to send prana into any painful area. You do this by directing your mind to channel energy to an area of your body. Again, if you try this, you will see that it works. The challenge is to keep your mind focused. With practice you can become more and more proficient.

Prana is considered normal when your breath is deep and full and your body is clean, light, supple, and vital. When prana is well developed, you have the ability to listen attentively, to comprehend many viewpoints, and to be able to take action appropriately.

Practices to keep your channels open to available prana are: nasal cleansing (neti) and nasal oiling (nasya), tongue scraping, eye washes, teeth cleaning, gum massage, oiling and massaging the ears, and body massage. Shirodhara, an Ayurvedic therapy of pouring warm oil over your forehead, will calm your mind and invoke an experience of silent spaciousness. Shirodhara deeply relaxes your nervous system, pacifies vata, and slows the thinking; then a wave of peace commences to circulate all through your cerebral spinal fluid, calming your whole nervous system.

Meditations focusing on space, openness, or infinity will increase prana. Focus on the space between things. Wherever space is created, prana moves within it. The key to creating energy is to create space. Once the space is created, the energy of Spirit will come forth. Even just creating space in your day to simply BE ... especially in nature, is an invitation for more prana (LIFE FORCE) to come through you.

Mindfulness meditation and the simple awareness of things as they are allows resistance to drop away and opens a lot of space. This practice of presence develops spaciousness for more prana to flow and for the receptive awareness of your heart to be developed. All space is sacred. Sacred is the nature of space!

One of the best things to focus on in mindfulness practice is the breath itself. Putting a simple sound on the breath is a beautiful, calming practice as well as a powerful practice to focus the power of your mind. Try this right now...

Inhale 'So' ... Exhale 'Hum' ...

'So' means I AM. 'Hum' means THAT, meaning all that is. This beautiful mantra fosters resting in ONENESS. Very calming for the mind and nervous system, it allows prana to flow wherever it is needed. It is in the practice of quieting and focusing your mind that a space is created for life force to rush in. There are mantras in every tradition and culture of the world. Chanting is a beautiful pathway to create more spaciousness in your mind.

Tejas – the most subtle form of pitta dosha

Tejas is the subtle energy of fire. It is the light within agni and pitta.

Fire, being upward moving, signifies your will and aspiration to know Divine Truth. When your mind is stable and discernment is clear and confident, the light of tejas burns clean and pure.

Tejas gives you intelligence, reason, passion to learn and discover, the power of self-discipline, and an increased ability to perceive things clearly. Tejas is the essence of speech. Speaking and articulating clearly increases your tejas, and the ability to speak clearly reflects a highly developed tejas. Confused speech disperses tejas and reflects a poorly developed tejas.

The activity of gossip is devastating to tejas. The words you listen to are feeding your tejas, and the words you speak are expressing your tejas. It is important for the development of tejas to understand what you hear in order to develop the capacity to discern truth from falsehood. It is also vital to live your truth, to do what you say and say what you do, and do things when and how you say you will. Your words should be clear and truthful and also sweet and gentle to develop tejas properly.

When tejas becomes too high, you direct judgment and criticism at yourself and/or others. You overly digest impressions and negate your experiences in life. Nothing can satisfy you. Doubt, anger, and irritability arise. Physical symptoms may include headaches, delirium, or burning in the head or eyes.

When tejas is too low, there is a tendency to become gullible and lose your ability to make choices that serve your highest aspirations. You become mentally passive and fall under the domination or influence of others. You may lack purpose and direction in life. When the mind is moving too fast or too slow, or your ability to discriminate is clouded by subconscious impressions (samskara) or emotion, tejas is impaired.

As you develop tejas, you will be able to see things as they are without the veil of opinions, judgments, likes, and dislikes of the conditioned mind. In this way you discover a reality that transcends appearances or meanings that are relative to your point of view.

Ojas - the most subtle form of kapha dosha

Ojas is the most material of the three subtle doshas and the most subtle form of kapha. Ojas provides support for prana and tejas. It is also the essence of the seven tissue layers of your body (called dhatus) and is sometimes considered the most subtle dhatu. It is the vital energy of life, your immune system, and your nervous system. Bri. Maya Tiwari says ojas is "The lubricating nectar within the physical organism."

The Dhatus are:

Rasa - Plasma and lymph
Rakta - Red blood cells
Mamsa - Muscle tissue
Medas - Fat tissue
Asthi - Bone
Majja - Bone marrow and nervous system
Asthi/Shukra - Sperm/ovum
Ojas - Subtle essence

Ojas is the subtle essence of vitality behind your immune and nervous systems. It is the stabilizing force beneath your mind and body. It is the prime energy reserve of your body. Ojas is also the energy that creates your aura and determines its strength against harmful energies.

On the psychological level, ojas is responsible for compassion, unconditional love, peace, and creativity. The ability to focus your mind allows ojas to be concentrated. Any practice that stabilizes your mind aids in increasing ojas. Ojas can be transformed into spiritual strength through any practice of devotion, pranayam, massage, and/or meditation.

Normal ojas is reflected in a strong immune system, steady calm emotions, patience, fearlessness, compassion, and endurance.

Excess ojas can lead one to be overly content, rigid, unwilling to learn new things or to grow. The mind becomes heavy and dull.

Deficient ojas can lead to low self-esteem, loss of confidence, nervous system exhaustion, mental breakdown, weak immune function, unstable mind and emotions, insomnia, heightened sensitivity to all stimuli, fear, worry, emaciation, or any symptom of high prana or tejas (or both). Ojas is increased through diet, tonic herbs, appropriate use of sexual energy, and spiritual practice. Its physical component is vital to its existence.

Factors which weaken ojas:

- Poor diet
- Environmental toxins
- Emotional abuse/trauma
- Drug/alcohol use
- Excessive or deficient sense stimulation
- Exposure to excess noise stimulation, TV, radio, bright lights, computers, cell phones
- Overindulgence in sex, lack of sexual contact, or sex without love
- Inadequate breathing
- Over-attachment
- Lack of love
- Forgetting our true nature as spirit

Ojas is depleted more easily than prana or tejas. Ojas is lost by excessive physical, mental, or emotional activity. Emotional strain and agitation are the very worst, particularly worry and anxiety. Disease, stress, excess travel, physical or mental overwork, or too much exercise deplete ojas. Too much exposure to harsh elements and excessive social contact can also lower ojas.

Factors which build ojas:

- Optimal nourishment and digestion
- Getting enough rest
- Nourishing sensory input
- Meditation
- Conscious breathing practices
- Chanting, singing
- Love, faith, and compassion
- Massage & loving touch
- Creating beauty/art in all forms
- Selfless service
- Gentle asana practice
- Colors: gold, yellow, blue, green, white, rose, violet
- Aromas: basil, rose, sandalwood, saffron, frankincense, lavender, lotus

Any work you engage in with the attitude of service and devotion will help build strength of character and nurture the flower of compassion in your heart, indicating an increase in ojas.

In Tantric practice, where the lover becomes the focus of spiritual devotion, loving touch and arousal can actually increase ojas, provided the sexual energy is perceived as spiritual nectar. This is a deep practice of intimacy, tenderness, love, and patience. The loss of excess sexual fluids is ojas-depleting.

Nurture yourself. Cultivate love, compassion, patience, devotion, and service in your life. Nourish yourself with fresh ojas-rich foods, herbs, rest, thoughts, enough (but not too much) exercise, and loving relations.

Food is very important for developing ojas, as ojas is the end product of food.

Ojas-increasing foods include:

- Ghee
- Raw honey
- Dates
- Raw milk (warm and spiced)
- Almonds
- Sesame seeds
- Cashews
- Coconut
- Organic, cold-pressed oils (coconut, olive, sunflower, sesame)
- Avocado
- Whole organic grains
- Sweet fruits
- Saffron

Dr. Vasant Lad suggests eating dates soaked in ghee to quickly build ojas.

Healthy oils will nourish and lubricate your tissues. Fat relates to love. Love yourself physically with warm oil massage and fats in your diet. You will become more juicy.

All foods should be fresh, organic, and prepared lovingly. All foods should be eaten in a sacred way, consciously, to provide ojas.

Ojas-increasing herbs are the rasayana (rejuvenative) herbs like:

- Shatavari
- Ashwagandha
- Brahmi
- Licorice
- Guduchi
- Amlaki
- Bala
- Shilajit
- Shanka Pushpi

Chyavanprash is excellent for nourishing ojas.

Superfoods also nourish ojas. Some examples are:

- Maca
- Seed and nut milks
- Bee pollen
- Royal jelly
- Elderberry/blueberry/blackberry
- Cacao
- Spirulina

Rest, sleep, and deep peaceful meditation increase ojas.

The true self is pure consciousness that transcends all conditions and circumstances. The path of knowing this true self requires discernment and self-observation. As understanding dawns on you, prana, tejas, and ojas are increased. You become a clear, light expression of love.

CHAPTER SIX

An Invitation to Practice

Engaging in a cleanse at least twice a year (and no more than 4 times per year, at the turn of the seasons) will do much to maintain your health and well-being as well as reorient you towards your highest aspirations for your life. You may also be preventing disease processes in a very real way.

According to Ayurveda, the 6 stages of dis-ease are:

- Accumulation (of doshas/ama)
- Aggravation (provocation)
- Overflow (from their site of origin)
- Relocation (to the weakest site of the body)
- Manifestation (identified as disease)
- Differentiation (chronic disease, complications)

Notice that the manifestation of disease is actually the fifth stage of a disease scenario. One of the great blessings of Ayurveda is cultivating your awareness to recognize subtle symptoms as clues to how you are out of balance so you can adjust your actions to disrupt, rebalance, and reverse this process before it has a chance to progress and manifest as a disease.

Seasonal cleansing practices could be vital in disrupting the progression of a disease. If you are grappling with a disease that has already manifested, it's important to be working with a skilled medical professional to address it in the best possible way.

Your body is an astounding organism, allowing you to experience all life has to offer. It is a highly sensitive organism that can hear, touch, see, taste, smell, express, act, feel, and transform energy from one form to another. How amazing is that?

When your agni (the digestive fire, including the ability to digest information and experience) is normal, it sustains your life, vitality, and optimum health. Agni is the fire element that works on many levels of your body-mind organism. Agni in the mind can also be seen as the light of perception, which helps you to discern reality. It is the fire of will that supports you in making clear choices. It is the fire in the belly that allows you to digest food and transform it into energy. There are many other agnis in the body as well that relate to the process of transforming substance into energy. In the West, we think of this process as metabolism, although agni is more clearly understood as the fire, or energy, that drives proper metabolism. When agni is sufficient, the mind, body, and senses will be clear and energized. You will have the ability and force to move your life in positive directions. You will be able to make supportive choices and transform anything you take into the body into life force, easily eliminating waste products.

There are many factors which can cause disruption in healthy metabolism. Some examples are eating lifeless "food," stress of all kinds, unsupportive lifestyle habits, not being fully present, and repressed or tumultuous emotions, especially when eating. These conditions do not allow for the transformation of what we receive through the senses into energy and healthy tissues.

When there is incomplete processing of food, thoughts, emotions, interactions, media input, pollutants, etc., the channels of your body, both physically and subtly, can become clogged with a thick, sticky, foul-smelling substance that is called ama in Ayurveda. Ama is most often described as a result of incomplete digestion of food or other information received through the senses. Ama is produced in your body in response to input from the environment that you cannot fully process. Examples are lifeless, processed food-like substances or toxins from any number of sources: pharmaceutical drugs, herbicides, pesticides, household products, body care products. It can also manifest from incomplete emotional processing of our life experiences, resulting in the accumulation of "molecules of emotion."

Molecules of emotion is a term that was coined by Candace Pert, PhD, describing the internally generated chemicals that bind to certain cell receptors all over the system, turning them on or off. An emotional revelation or release can actually reverse the course of a dis-ease that is in process. Habitual thoughts and behaviors that generate supportive feeling-states actually create new neural pathways in your brain and throughout your body. Remember, you are continually regenerating your body-mind organism!

According to Ayurveda, ama is the root cause of many diseases. When the subtle channels of your body are clogged with ama, tiredness, heaviness, and/or a sense of fogginess ensues. Some signs of ama in your system are constipation, indigestion, excess gas, diarrhea, bad breath, strong body odor, coated tongue, body aches and pains, stiffness, confusion, or a feeling of being "stuck."

A highly functioning digestive fire (agni) will reduce the formation of ama in your body. This fire can be increased with regular use of pungent spices like ginger, cloves, peppers, cinnamon, garlic, and onions. Your digestive fire can be balanced accordingly (either increasing or decreasing agni) with the use of cumin, coriander, and fennel seeds. These spices are used liberally in Ayurvedic cooking. You can also make a tea with these seeds, or they can be roasted and chewed on following meals for improved digestion.

Mental ama is as crippling to the system as physical ama. Mental ama is accumulated as a result of unresolved issues, misperceptions, judgments, and disturbed thoughts. Emotions such as greed, fear, selfishness, possessiveness, and anger convert to mental pollution or ama. Mental ama can have a destructive influence on your digestion and may convert even wholesome foods into ama. According to Ayurveda, all internally generated disease begins with an accumulation of ama in your organism. All diseases caused by external influences produce ama in your organism.

The cleansing practices outlined here are specifically designed to loosen, melt, and eliminate ama from your body, mind, and all subtle channels of your system. Using oils, both internally and externally, you are directly addressing ama or fat-soluble toxins, the specific toxic substances which are stored in fat cells (this includes heavy metals and "candida," pesticides, plastic residues, and more).

Gentle cleansing at the juncture of the seasons, when you feel the most susceptible, will help keep toxins from accumulating and keep your metabolism strong. Accumulated excesses are most easily moved at the juncture of the seasons, as everything in nature is in flux. Your body experiences everything that is happening in the natural world, as you are an integral part of it.

At the end of summertime, you may have accumulated excess heat; at the end of fall, excess wind and dryness; at the end of winter, excess coldness; and at the end of spring, excess dampness. You are also more susceptible to dis-ease at these times when all things are in the midst of change.

Cyclical cleansing can greatly support your body and mind immediately and over time. It is a gift you can give yourself of lightening up, refreshing your heart, clearing your mind, and re-orienting toward your highest visions and goals. Regular cleansing also enhances the beneficial effects of any foods, tonics, or herbal medicines because your tissues are open and more receptive and capable of absorbing and assimilating more effectively following a cleanse.

Please remember that cleansing is not right for everyone at all times. This cleansing practice in particular reaches very deeply into your whole organism. It is only to be embarked upon if and when you are feeling strong. It should be approached with great respect and support. It is strongly recommended to work with an Ayurvedic practitioner to determine the right treatments, herbs, and foods specific for you, at least the first time you embark on this profound cleanse.

CHAPTER SEVEN

Panchakarma Foundations

There are three distinct stages of the cleansing practices introduced herein. The first is preparing your body and mind for releasing easily without damaging your body in any way. The second stage includes the main cleansing practices, and the third is a specific time and focus for conscious rejuvenation. In Ayurveda, these three aspects are called purvakarma, panchakarma, and rasayana.

To prepare your body for gentle release, Ayurveda uses oiling and sweating. Oiling your body, externally and internally, starts to loosen and liquefy ama (which is fat soluble) from the tissue structure. It softens and opens the tissues and lubricates all of the channels in your body so that when your body is heated up and subtle channels are dilated, accumulations can flow from where they have been held (commonly joints, organs, and brain) to the natural channels of elimination: your skin, bowel, and bladder.

There are 5 specific cleansing actions that are used in traditional Ayurvedic cleansing, panchakarma (PK).

Basti: An herbalized or oil enema to eliminate excess dryness, gas, and weakness from the colon, low back, and the bones.

Basti is most effective for constipation, low back pain, joint pain or stiffness, anxiety, headaches, viral symptoms, sexual dysfunction, and many other vata type symptoms. The main site or seat of vata in the body is the large intestine (aka colon).

Virechana: A thorough purge of the small intestine, liver, and gall bladder to release excess heat and bile; also to cleanse the blood, liver, spleen, and sweat glands. Releasing excess heat from the body can also help to balance your hormonal system, benefit your skin, and improve your eyesight. Virechana is specific for removing excess pitta. The main seat of pitta is the small intestine, with the liver being another main pitta organ.

Nasya: A cleansing of the nasal passages, the doorway to your brain. Nasya clears excesses from your sinuses, both physically and energetically, bringing increased clarity of mind and improved vision and hearing, reducing the predilection for allergies and headaches.

Vamana: Therapeutic emesis to remove excess mucous from your stomach and lungs. (It is not so commonly practiced in the U.S., but when needed, is profound.)

Rakta Moksha: The literal translation is liberation of blood, and it refers to blood cleansing. Bloodletting is still used today in India to relieve the blood of excess heat/fire/acidity. Some practitioners in the West recommend even donating blood for this purpose. I like to use blood cleansing herbs and foods to alkalize the system, as well as conscious breathing practices, massage, herbs, and exercise to stimulate the lymphatic system and oxygenate the blood. These practices reduce excess pitta in the blood.

While this book is a manual for teaching and empowering you to be able to engage in your own seasonal cleansing practices, it is still much more beneficial to engage in a retreat panchakarma when possible and allow a skilled practitioner to minister these therapies to you. "The deeper you go, the deeper you get" while doing these practices, and if you can let go of all of the preparations and "doing" and just receive, you can drop into deeper layers of relaxation (and perhaps) revelation.

Being on a personal retreat allows you an experience of totally letting go and being nurtured by daily treatments. The therapies used in Ayurveda are used not only to prepare your body and mind for deep and safe release, but also to induce a state of deep peace. Being in retreat, away from the patterns, habits, and demands of your daily life, helps you to see where you may have resistance and also allows you to remember your natural state of bliss and joy. Ideally, you are immersed in a beautiful setting in nature, and your practitioner is holding you in a safe and sacred space. Your meals are prepared for you, allowing you to rest deeply, be in silence if you like, engage in spiritual practice, process emotions that arise, and simply be.

Besides the basic oiling and sweating practices, Ayurveda uses many elaborate and luxurious therapies during a panchakarma retreat that take you deeper into your experience by flooding your senses with beauty and delight. These exotic therapies all have a precise purpose as well. I will describe a few, just to give you a sense of how profoundly beautiful this art (and science) is.

Abhyanga is the applying of warm oils to your skin to start loosening ama from your tissues, increase circulation, increase lymph movement, soften and smooth your skin, stimulate your organs, and lubricate your joints. During panchakarma you will typically receive an hour and a half abhyanga daily, traditionally ministered by two therapists to re-establish the proper flows of prana in your body. This massage is invigorating and relaxing at the same time. When you receive from two therapists, your brain cannot track all that is happening and your mind just has to let go. It is heavenly. See page 107 for self-anointing ritual instructions.

Swedana refers to sweating therapies. During a panchakarma retreat we use several methods, most commonly a steam tent that goes right over the massage table following your massage. We use either fresh herbs or pure essential oils chosen to enhance the experience and bring about balance specifically for you. We also use hot towels and boluses filled with herbs or other healing concoctions to heat your tissues, move energy, and encourage release of toxins.

Shirodhara is a treatment usually ministered after a warm oil massage. During shirodhara your body is carefully adjusted into a perfectly comfortable position for you to be able to totally relax and let go. Then, a stream of warm oil is slowly and gently poured back and forth over your forehead for at least a half hour, more as indicated. Shirodhara is deeply stress-relieving and pacifies vata dosha while nourishing and calming your nervous system. This treatment transports you into a deeply meditative state of being. Shirodhara activates your hypothalamus and pituitary glands, heightening spiritual awareness and bringing more balance to your hormonal system. It can also cleanse your mind and senses of held impressions and improve your mental clarity and cognition. Shirodhara is classically indicated for stress, anxiety, worry, insomnia, memory loss, headaches, adrenal exhaustion, emotional imbalance, and any imbalance of your head, neck, eyes, ears, nose, and nervous system.

Another one of the treatments often ministered during a retreat panchakarma is called udvartana. Udvartana is an herbalized scrub that gets applied after a warm oil massage and before the steam immersion. The exfoliating paste is applied in an upward movement toward the heart to stimulate the movement of lymph. This is Ayurveda's premier therapy for weight loss, as it breaks up cellulite and excess accumulation in fat cells. It also leaves the skin feeling like velvet! Everyone loves this treatment whether they desire to lose weight or not. The benefits of moving the lymph and stimulating and exfoliating the skin are many and undeniably delicious.

There are specific treatments for addressing your eyes, nose, ears, joints, and skin. There is even a full-body oil "bath" called pizhichil, where warm oils are poured continuously over your body. This treatment was reserved for the royalty in Ancient India. It is deeply nourishing for anyone and specific for anyone with dryness, stiffness, or pain in their body. This therapy is pure bliss ... and deeply de-toxifying.

Panchakarma can be administered in a very matter of fact, medically focused way or also as a profound ceremony of anointing and remembrance of your Divine nature and wholeness. Choose a practitioner accordingly.

Diving Deep into Sacred Space

For some people, the depth of tenderness and intimacy they experience while receiving these therapies brings up deeply held issues of worthiness. It's my primary intention to affirm a sense of unquestionable worthiness and to anoint the Divine Being that lives through you.

It is highly beneficial to do a retreat PK once a year at your most vulnerable time of the year, and/or a self-administered cleanse at least one other time during each year. If you cannot take a retreat time with a practitioner, try to do a home cleanse twice a year. The gift of radiant health is worth the investment in yourself!

Taking this time for yourself while consciously raising awareness of habitual patterns of thinking or states of mind allows emotions to arise into conscious awareness for witnessing and releasing.

Clearing trapped emotions from your body or the field can be as simple as this: Making a space and consciously inviting them to reveal themselves. If you can accept these passing emotions and witness them without attachment to a story or blame, this can allow emotional patterns to release. If you have a lot of emotional issues, it is highly beneficial to allow a trusted practitioner to support you through this, or any, cleanse.

Create Space for an Optimal Experience

There are many ways to promote a deeper experience while cleansing:

- If you can, plan your cleanse at a time when you can let go of work and/or your normal everyday duties.
- Rest as much as possible.
- Surround yourself with beauty, flowers, candles, or anything that makes you feel a sense of the sacredness in what you're doing.
- Sit in meditation or quiet contemplation upon rising, after your treatments, and in the evening.
- Practice gentle body awareness with movement, yoga, qigong, walking, or swimming.
- Open to the life force (prana) available in nature.
- Be silent, listen within.
- Avoid extremes.
- Eat in a calm manner.
- Consciously open your senses and feel your body.
- Become the observer to the mind's endless ramblings (and ask, "who is observing?").
- Allow memories and the emotional response to them to arise gently for simple witnessing and releasing.
- Ask yourself often ... what nourishes me? What are the things I want to be doing for myself?
- What patterns of thinking, behavior, or habit keep me from the things I want to be doing for myself?
- Keep a journal of your insights during PK.

Here are a few things to reflect upon that may help you to know yourself better, or they may just open up more questions, and that's ok! We so often think we need to have all the answers to be safe or smart or loved. We don't.

See what happens for you on the inside when you ponder these ideas or questions. You could even choose one of these questions and reflect on it periodically for days or even weeks, months, or years...

- In what ways am I the creator of my own reality?
- All that is, arises from consciousness.
- All experience is for the purpose of raising awareness.
- The basis of life is freedom; the objective of life is joy; the result is expansion.
- Experience and awareness are the means for evolution to occur.
- Dis-ease is a transient, impersonal energy operating through a resonant channel.
- Taking full responsibility is a willingness and an ability to respond.
- We live in a vibrational universe.
- Appreciation and gratitude raise vibrational frequency.
- I can always accept and allow, or I can resist what IS.
- In any situation I can choose one of these heart virtues:

Appreciation
Compassion
Forgiveness
Generosity
Humility
Understanding
Valor

CHAPTER EIGHT

How Food Heals

"For anyone to remember the Soul, food is very essential.

From Divine Soul, Ether emerged.
From Ether came Air.
From Air was born Fire.
And from Fire came Water.
From Water, Earth emerged,
And from the Earth, various plants, and food.
Finally from food, human beings evolved.

The life principle present within our gross body (Annamaya Kosha) is called Prana.

Within the sheath of Prana (Pranamaya Kosha) is present the sheath of mind (Manomaya Kosha) and within it, the subtler sheath of intellect (Vijnanamaya Kosha). Latent in the Vijnanamaya Kosha is the sheath of bliss (Ananadamaya Kosha).

Many people stop journeying after reaching the Mind sheath. To attain bliss you must proceed onward, beyond food, mind, and the sheath of the intellect."

– Bhagavan Sri Sathya Sai Baba

The foods you choose and the way you eat have a profound effect on your well-being. I will give you an overview of the Ayurvedic food paradigm here and then many recipes in the healing recipes chapter (Chapter 15) for truly, food is our best medicine. I would love to help you remember the source and beauty of food as foundational for well-being and awaken your interest and delight in food so that you might have endless fun dreaming up delicious, creative meals, guided by your own senses and what you know is life-supporting for YOU.

Radiant health, like disease, is built day by day, it does not just happen. Diet is one of the most important factors for the promotion of health or the manifestation of disease. Food is essential for maintaining life. Your body is the product of food that is digested. I repeat, the health and integrity of your body depends on the nature of the food that you eat and how well it is digested.

It takes just 30 days for the food you eat to be converted into life-sustaining energy, called ojas, if digested and assimilated well. An upgrade in the quality of food you eat and adjusting your eating habits to be able to receive more nourishment from food will be reflected in overall increased vitality. Your natural immunity will be strengthened and your lightness of being will radiate.

Your state of consciousness directly affects how well you are able to digest and assimilate food. As you are choosing foods (especially for a cleanse), make sure you are getting the highest quality, fresh organic foods possible. If there is a local farmer's market, you can buy directly from a farmer. If not, most areas now have some kind of natural food store or even an organic section of a grocery store. The ideal is to eat the highest quality foods you can access in a state of gratitude for how this food is assisting you! Cultivating these habits in your daily life will promote better digestion and assimilation. Especially during your cleanse, observe these guidelines to enhance your experience.

Eating Habits

Your consciousness directly affects how well you transform the foods you eat into your physical tissues and energy field. This is true at all levels: the choosing of your foods, the preparation, the eating itself, and even awareness after meals to promote complete digestion.

How you eat can be even more important than what you eat. Less than ideal food eaten in a state of full presence and gratitude can be digested and assimilated more fully than the best of foods eaten in a disturbed or distracted state of mind. Eating when emotionally upset or when you're not really present can compromise digestion. This can result in gas, indigestion, perhaps heartburn, and the formation of ama. The ideal is to eat the highest quality foods in a relaxed and calm way to promote complete transformation of food into pure life force and healthy tissues.

Here are a few simple guidelines to help you maximize your digestion:

- Eat foods prepared by loving hands in a loving way.
- Make eating a sacred ritual. Take a moment to relax and give thanks before eating.
- Focus on eating consciously without distraction by television or computer, reading, driving, excessive conversation, or any other activities.
- Sit down when you eat. Eat in a pleasant, clean, calm setting. (No eating in the car!)
- Do not drink cold drinks just prior to eating or large amounts of water during mealtime. Doing so dampens the digestive fire.
- Chew your food well before swallowing.
- If you have a tendency to eat too fast or too much, put down your eating utensil between bites.
- Eat at a moderate pace until you are 75% full.

- Following meals, take a few minutes to relax and allow your food to digest.
- Take a leisurely walk for 10-15 minutes before resuming activity, or lie down on your left side and relax for a few minutes.
- Allow three hours between meals to allow your food to fully digest.

When you buy most Ayurvedic cookbooks, they are full of delicious Indian fare. As Ayurveda originated in India, this makes sense, but the theory behind the food preparation is what makes it Ayurvedic, not the ethnic style.

The most important factors in Ayurvedic food preparation are:

- Preparing the food with love and attention
- Eating only fresh, vital, organic, whole foods (no old food, no canned, frozen, boxed, or microwaved food)
- Eating foods in season grown in your region as much as possible
- Paying attention to food combinations
- Trying to include all six tastes in each meal; or, if you know which tastes are most balancing for you specifically, use more of those.

The Six Tastes

In the system of Ayurveda, there is not a focus on getting enough protein, carbohydrates, or particular vitamins. Instead, the way to achieve a balanced diet is by including all six tastes in every meal. The six tastes are:

~ sweet ~ sour ~ salty ~ bitter ~ pungent ~ astringent ~

- Sweet taste: Earth and Water
- Sour taste: Earth and Fire

- Salty taste: Water and Fire
- Pungent taste: Fire and Air
- Bitter taste: Ether and Air
- Astringent Taste: Air and Earth

The first three tastes (sweet, sour, and salty) naturally increase moisture in your body, decrease vata, and increase kapha. Therefore, they are considered building or tonifying.

The last three tastes (pungent, bitter, and astringent) have an opposite effect; they increase vata and reduce kapha. They are considered reducing or cleansing for different reasons. Pungent burns up ama while increasing metabolism. Astringent is drying and pulling. Bitter is the most cleansing and detoxifying, as the body wants to expel the bitter taste. Pitta is increased by sour, salty, and pungent tastes and is decreased by the sweet, bitter, and astringent tastes.

Sweet taste includes whole grains, nuts, sweet fruits and vegetables (yams, winter squash, carrots, etc.), honey, maple syrup, dairy, eggs, and meat. Sweet taste is what builds tissues.

Sour taste includes lemons, limes, grapefruit, tomatoes, yogurt, fermented foods, and sour fruits. Sour taste is warming.

Salty taste includes various kinds of salts and seaweeds. Find out the source of the salts and sea vegetables you are using. If the source is the sea, is it harvested from a clean source? Also, try using earth-based salts, such as Himalayan Salt. Salt is very important because it adds needed minerals and also moistens the body. Avoid using common commercial salt, as it has chemical additives to make it pour more easily.

Bitter taste includes all the leafy greens. We receive so much value from these foods, both raw and lightly cooked. However, vata types beware, bitter taste is the most cleansing (and cooling) for the tissues. Too much bitter taste can imbalance you.

Pungent taste includes hot peppers, ginger, black pepper, onions, garlic, cinnamon, and cloves. Pungent taste increases metabolism, promotes good circulation, and increases digestive fire (agni). Too much pungent taste can imbalance pitta types.

Astringent taste includes all legumes, pomegranate, turmeric, less than fully-ripe banana, green apples, and green tea. There is some astringency in cucumber and summer squash. You will feel that slight sensation of pulling in your mouth. Astringent taste is drying and absorbing.

Most Westerners focus almost exclusively on sweet, sour, and salty tastes. These foods are comforting and increase the tissues, leading to obesity. Bitter, pungent, and astringent tastes are more cleansing and are vital for a balanced physiology.

You will find that you are much more satisfied after eating food that includes all six tastes. You will need less food to be totally content. Please heighten this awareness and practice. It is vital to remember that health and strength are not only in the food but arise from your ability to digest and assimilate the food you eat and eliminate the waste products that are not needed by your body. Signs of difficulty digesting are excess gas, bloating after eating or constipation (vata), feeling any kind of burning sensation after eating, heartburn or acid indigestion or diarrhea (pitta), or heaviness or tiredness after eating (kapha.)

If you eat only when hungry and only eat what you can digest, you will feel light and satisfied with no signs of indigestion and have regular bowel movements 1-3 times per day. Food fuels, replenishes, and makes the digestive fire function properly. Agni, the digestive fire, is the first cause of good health, mental clarity, and spiritual radiance.

Take some time to reflect on these questions:

- What are your feelings about food?
- What is your inner story when you're eating?
- Do you have struggles with food?
- Do you have any difficulty digesting food? If so, what kinds of food and/or under what circumstances?

- What do you perceive as the cause(s) of the problem(s)?
- How can you tell when your body is hungry?
- How often do you eat when you are hungry and how often do you eat for other reasons?
- Why do you eat when you are not hungry?
- How often do you overeat?
- Why do you overeat?
- How can you tell what kinds of foods your body needs?
- How did you establish your present diet?
- Is your present diet similar to what your parents brought you up on?
- Are you satisfied with your present diet?
- What changes would you like to make and why?

In the West, we have been trained to think about food in terms of its chemical components (proteins, carbohydrates, fats, vitamins, and minerals.) In Ayurveda, food and nutrition are seen in terms of relationships. Food is a part of your total sensory experience and a link between your outer and inner environments. The first and foremost consideration is who it is that is going to eat.

Each of us is unique. Your diet needs to be based on what qualities will bring balance to you, as well as your digestive capacity and limitations. The specific quantity of a particular food that can be digested, assimilated, and excreted is related to your prakruti and vikruti, your occupation, the climate, season of the year, your stage of life, your state of mind, etc.

I will briefly introduce the basic ways that Ayurveda classifies food.

- **Taste/Rasa** – This refers to the six tastes: sweet, sour, salty, bitter, pungent, astringent
- **Energy/Virya** – Is it heating or cooling?
- **Qualities/Guna** – Is it heavy or light, moist or dry, etc.

- **Post-digestive effect/Vipaka** – Post-digestively, sweet and salty tastes become sweet; sour remains sour; and pungent, bitter, and astringent tastes become pungent. These relate to the post-digestive effects of absorption and elimination. Sweet effects increase kapha dosha. Sour effects increase pitta dosha. Pungent effects increase vata dosha.
- **Specific Action/Prabhav** – This is a unique effect of a particular food (that may not fit into the above considerations). For example: Honey, while being sweet, you would expect it to be cooling, but it is heating. Ginger is pungent, its virya is heating, however its vipak (post-digestive effect) is sweet. There are other exceptions, but for the most part you can use your senses alone to discern the qualities of foods.

In a life-changing workshop for me with Bri. Maya Tiwari called "Food, Breath, & Sound," she took us to a large natural food store and walked right over to the produce section. She picked up an avocado and asked us, "What do you know about this food? Is it heavy or light? Oily or dry? Sweet? Salty? Sour? Bitter? Pungent? Astringent?" Of course, we said it was heavy, oily, sweet. So, who does it balance? VATA! Who does it imbalance? Kapha! Then, she walked over to a bunch of dark green leafy kale and asked us the same questions. To which we answered: it is light, dry, and bitter. YES! And who does it balance? Kapha! Imbalances vata! Right! How about this cayenne pepper? Hot, light, dry ... Imbalances pitta, right? Melon? cool, sweet, heavy, and wet ... Balancing for pitta. What a glorious and memorable moment when I realized, "Yes. I'm getting this."

This went on and on until we were really sensing the qualities of each of the vegetables, grains, beans, and spices. It was so great! So liberating! I never had very much luck memorizing all those lists of V, P, and K foods. Not to mention that there are contradictions in the lists from different sources. This gave me the tools to look at all foods through new eyes. Looking at food this way engages your senses and your mind (and elevates your consciousness). You have to really be present and aware to make these determinations. No more simply choosing out of habit or ignorance. Very very valuable.

The digestive fire is said to be the strongest at mid-day, when the sun is the highest in the sky (between 10 AM and 2 PM). Try having a simple but nourishing meal for breakfast, your largest meal at lunchtime, and a lighter meal in the evening. Eating a lighter meal in the evening will allow the liver to detoxify more thoroughly at night. During the cleanse, skip breakfast if you can and just have hot water with lemon, ginger tea, or a blood cleansing tea.

The cleanse outlined in this book uses specific foods and herbs to assist the cleansing process. The main food is called kitchari, (also spelled kichadi, kichari, kicharee, or kitcharee depending on region). It is considered the most healing food in Ayurveda. I have witnessed many people bring their digestion and eating habits into a healthy, balanced state by simply eating kitchari for a period of time. It is a wonderfully satisfying food because it includes all six tastes. The palate and the cells are truly delighted by this food. It is delicious. It is also a complete protein, loaded with vegetables and spices, all of which promote and enhance digestion.

In this cleanse, you are specifically and intentionally keeping the digestion functioning and using it to naturally nourish and cleanse the tissues of your body. The astringency of the kitchari acts like a sponge to absorb the toxins that are being released through the other methods you are using. The kitchari provides fibrous bulk which scrubs your intestinal wall and keeps everything moving.

According to Ayurveda, kitchari is the preferred food to use when on a mono-diet or when fasting. It is excellent for detoxification and de-aging of the cells. It is also very calming to the mind and body to simply have one easily-digested food for a period of time. We don't realize how much mental and emotional energy is tied up in our food choices.

Food can be a supreme medicine when prepared with awareness. In the kitchari recipe in chapter 15, I use only whole or freshly ground spices. When the spices are whole, they still contain all of the life force. If planted, they would grow. When they are ground, they release their prana right away. Please don't waste your dollars on pre-ground spices. They lack life force, aroma, and flavor!

If you want to use ground spices, grind them yourself and use them within about a week's time. First dry roast a handful of whole coriander or cumin seeds (I will often roast them together). Put the seeds into a dry frying pan and toast over medium to low heat until you smell the aromas being released from the seeds, remove from the stove right away, and grind with a mortar and pestle or a coffee grinder used only for spices and herbs.

These are the primary spices used in most Ayurvedic cooking and their qualities:

Mustard seed (warming)
Cumin (balancing)
Coriander (balancing)
Ginger (warming, though fresh ginger is cooler)
Turmeric (warming)
Fennel (cooling)
Cardamom (warming)
Fenugreek (cooling)
Asafetida (warming & gas reducing)
Basil (warming)
Cilantro (cooling)
Chile peppers (heating)

According to Ayurveda, continued good health is dependent upon your capacity to fully metabolize the nutritional, emotional, and sensory information that you ingest. When your digestive energies (agnis) are robust, you create healthy tissues, eliminate wastes efficiently, and produce the subtle essence called ojas. Ojas, the innermost sap of your psycho-physiology, is the basis for your clarity of perception, physical strength, and immunity. On the other hand, if your agnis are weakened, digestion is incomplete, resulting in the accumulation of toxic residue, ama. Ama and agni have opposing qualities. Remember, ama is cold, heavy, cloudy, malodorous, sticky, and impure. Agni is hot, dry, clear, light, fragrant, and pure.

Ama is the root cause of many diseases. If you are able to cyclically remove ama from your system, you will also noticeably reduce your propensity to get "colds," fevers, allergies, or arthritis. How great is that?

Nutritional Approaches to Reducing Ama

This is worth repeating: According to Ayurveda, the quality of food, the type of food, the means of taking food, and the environment in which the food is eaten all influence your ability to thoroughly digest a meal. If the conditions support the healthy functioning of agni, strong tissues are created, and ojas permeates your psycho-physiology. If however, the digestive fires are not functioning optimally, food is incompletely metabolized and ama is created.

Ama-Reducing Diet: Recommended Food Choices During a Home Cleanse

- All foods should be freshly prepared, nutritious, and appetizing. Canned foods and leftovers should be avoided
- Foods should be lighter in quality, such as rice, soups, and lentils
- Favor freshly steamed or very lightly sautéed vegetables
- Avoid fried foods
- Avoid cold food and drinks
- Dairy products should be avoided or minimized
- Avoid fermented foods and drinks

- Oils should be kept to a minimum
- Lighter grains such as quinoa, millet, buckwheat, basmati rice, or barley should be favored
- Refined sugars should be avoided. Small amounts of honey may be used, but never heated. Small amounts of maple syrup are preferred for a more cooling sweetener
- Most oily, heavy nuts should be avoided. Small quantities of sunflower, sesame, or pumpkin seeds may be taken
- Avoid animal products. If you must eat meat, favor white chicken or turkey. Avoid all red meat and pork

Recommended Tastes and Spices

Bitter and pungent tastes are the most useful to treat ama. Bitter taste reduces ama and pungent destroys it. Sweet, salty, and sour tastes may aggravate ama and should be reduced. Astringent taste is generally neutral in its effect on ama.

Bitter spices including turmeric and coriander are useful. Warm spices such as cumin, cardamom, basil, and fennel are balancing and will not aggravate pitta. The hot spices such as cayenne, black pepper, dry ginger, and mustard are very useful in burning up ama but must be used cautiously if pitta is aggravated. Fresh ginger is not as heating as the dry form and should be used generously.

Duration of the Ama-Reducing Diet

Although many of the general principles of the ama-reducing diet are beneficial at all times, the prohibitions against dairy, oils, nuts, and heavier grains can be lifted once the signs and symptoms of ama have dissipated. Small, occasional servings of fermented foods, fried foods, and sweeteners can also then be taken.

The ama-reducing diet is recommended three times a year at the change of the seasons. People with predominantly vata constitutions should follow the diet for 1-2 weeks. People with pitta constitutions may follow it for up to 1 month. Those with kapha constitutions can tolerate the ama-reducing program for longer periods of time as it is most closely related to the kapha pacifying regimen.

It is very important that you are cooking in non-toxic cookware. Please avoid cooking in aluminum or teflon-coated pans. There are some new "green" non-stick pans that are non-toxic. Also stainless steel, glass, cast iron, clay, and stoneware are all non-toxic.

CHAPTER NINE

Additional Practices to Enhance Your Cleanse

There are many ways to enhance your experience during a seasonal cleanse.

Here are some suggestions that may inspire you. Most of these come from the yogic tradition, of which Ayurveda is a sister science.

Rehydration Drink

Sip hot water every 15 - 20 minutes to rehydrate your cells; or make a pot of mint and/or tulsi tea and add juice from ½ of a lime and a small amount of raw sugar (cooling) or honey (warming) and a pinch of Himalayan salt.

Sip throughout the day.

Bath with Epsom Salts

In a bath of Epsom salts and baking soda, practice conscious breathing to pump the lymphatic system. I have heard this may aid in removing heavy metals from the body as well.

Neti - Nasal Rinse

In the yogic system, there are several different methods for cleansing the nasal passages. This will clear your sinuses, calm and open your mind, and improve the flow of prana, life force. I will speak only of jala neti or water cleansing. This is a wonderful, safe treatment, particularly if you have allergies or headaches.

To purchase a neti pot, see Resources, starting on page 183.

Fill your neti pot with lukewarm water. Add about ⅛ tsp. of salt to ½ cup water or ¼ tsp. for 1 cup water. The water should be about the same saltiness as ocean water. This saline level is what we have in our own bodies, and with the right balance of salt, your neti should be very pleasant and easy, avoiding that sensation of water up your nose!

NOTE: USE ONLY HIGHEST QUALITY SALT: Himalayan pink salt, real earth salt, or sea salt from a clean source. DO NOT USE IODIZED TABLE SALT (for anything).

Standing over a sink or outside tilt your head down and turn it to one side.

Close off the back of your throat with your tongue. Put the spout into the upper nostril and tip the neti pot so the water starts to flow into it. You should feel your sinus cavity fill up, and the water will start to pour out through the lower nostril. Repeat on the other side. This takes a little practice and getting used to, but it's a wonderful practice for those with any sinus issues, sore throats, headaches, and allergies. If you have inflammation in the sinuses, (indicated by chronic irritation, redness, or infections) you may want to try adding a little turmeric to the water.

Trataka - Flame Meditation

Trataka is a simple practice for cleansing and strengthening your eyes. It will also calm your mind and nervous system as well as improve your visual capacity. It may also be helpful for headaches and nervous conditions.

Place a candle or ghee lamp at eye level about 3 feet from your eyes. Sit in a comfortable posture with your spine erect and simply gaze at the flame without blinking your eyes as much as possible. Try to ignore any watering or discomfort that arises. Start out with 30 seconds and add 10 seconds per week. You will notice that your gaze becomes much more steady and your mind very calm.

Make a rinse for your eyes with pure organic rose water, chrysanthemum tea, or triphala tea. Be sure to strain it very well!

Tune in to sunrise and sunset times. If you can, gaze at the rising and setting sun. This is also a great time to meditate.

Asana Practices for Different Types

The seat of vata (air) is the colon, and its main sites in the body are from the colon down, including the reproductive organs, low back, hips, legs, and feet, as well as the nervous system. Vata types mostly need to calm the nervous system, still the mind, and also compress the colon (the seat of vata) to release any excess gas. So any sitting posture, balance postures, and anything that compresses the lower belly and stretches out the low back, hips, and legs can be beneficial.

The seat of pitta (fire) is the small intestine. The liver and gall bladder are also major pitta organs. So the whole mid-section of the body, the organ cavity, is where pitta is concentrated. Pitta types will benefit most from postures that stimulate and squeeze the main digestive organs. So, compressing the belly as in the child's pose or bow pose or spinal twists of all kinds will be beneficial.

Kapha (water/earth) is located in the upper stomach, lungs, neck, and head. Kapha types need to stretch open the lungs and ribs, shoulders and neck, freeing the upper body of any stagnation. Good poses for Kapha will include reaching the arms above the head, bridge pose, camel pose, side bends, and back bends.

Any posture where your head is below your heart or your feet are above your heart is very beneficial for pumping your lymphatic system. A simple forward bend, bringing your belly and chest towards your thighs and your head down, hands to feet, is helpful. Bend your knees a little if you need or want to. Spend some time in this position, or if it's too uncomfortable to do for long, return to it often. Just be present in this posture. Notice your breath and allow it to open your low back and legs. Note: If you can't do this in a standing position, try doing it sitting in a chair.

Another very simple one is to lie on your back and lift your legs up to a 90 degree angle. Just rest there as long as you can. You may want to try using a strap to hold your feet up, rest your lower legs on a chair, or put your legs up a wall. No need to strain. Allow gravity to move your lymph and clean your blood!

Resource for free yoga videos for all levels:
www.DoYogaWithMe.com

- Give yourself permission to rest as much as you need to, and be in bed by 10:00 PM at the latest.
- Do gentle yoga asanas, tai chi, Qi gong, or stretching with heightened awareness and presence.
- Do lymphatic pumping asanas (inverted postures).
- Walk in full presence.
- Spend as much time as possible in silence.
- Be in nature and receive all the beauty and life force constantly available.
- Keep your time open and spacious, your focus inward.
- Expand JOYFULNESS with gratitude and awareness.
- Eat with full presence, slowly, quietly, with a grateful heart.
- Focus on the tastes, aromas, colors, and textures of the food you are eating.

CHAPTER TEN

Our Beautiful Emotions - Energy in Motion

When most people think of a cleanse, they tend to think of a physical detoxification (in all of its gory details). Let us expand the perception of a cleanse beyond the physical body to include your whole being. To simply cleanse from busy-ness for a week each season would benefit anyone. To cleanse from automatic or learned eating habits would be of great benefit. To cleanse from media input – the computer, TV, newspapers, and magazines would eliminate a lot of stress that is received through the senses.

In Chapter 6, I mentioned ama, the sticky substance that results from the incomplete processing of thoughts, feelings, emotions, or any sensory input. Unprocessed energies held in your body or auric field forge subtle energy pathways that can keep you stuck in limiting patterns. These patterns could be belief systems, ways of thinking, behaviors, or reactions to stress that are not life-promoting.

It has been said that 90% of all illness, injury, and emotional trauma is caused by stress. All stress is caused by some combination of environmental factors, dietary factors, or the mental and emotional responses to the experiences we take in through the senses. It's also worth remembering that up to 95% of our responses to input are generated in the subconscious mind. The subconscious mind is developed in early childhood by the input received from others. So, unless we take time to clear the subconscious mind, there are patterns running that were learned from others and which are no longer relevant to who we are now.

Your body is your most intimate feedback system. It plays out and brings into reality every thought and belief you have. Every cell in your body is constantly listening to and responding to every bit of information it is receiving from the environment. Every thought, every feeling, every attitude, every perception of every bit of input received through your senses is constantly communicating with your DNA.

In the field of epigenetics, researchers are discovering more and more evidence that your attitude determines the nature of the electromagnetic signals that reach your DNA. According to research done by Dr. Bruce Lipton, a negative frame of mind generates a certain frequency impulse throughout your body, and the DNA responds to this signal by shutting down specific hormonal pathways in the brain that perpetuate this feeling state.

When you are able to observe your own attitudes and consciously break the pattern, by laughing at it or being curious about it, for example, the signal is changed into a completely different frequency, which then activates a different set of hormonal pathways that perpetuate well-being. This is so exciting to me!

Every experience, every thought, every emotion, and every word you say or hear is communicating with every cell in your body. Each one of us has a choice to wake up and take 100% responsibility for regulating the input that we encounter in life. When an individual becomes more aware, it's possible to start seeing patterns and asking questions like, "Who says that?" "Is that something I learned from my mother, father, culture, TV?" "Is that true?" "What else is possible?"

In every circumstance you experience, there is opportunity to choose an evolutionary perspective that elevates you to more freedom and expansion. Even when potent things happen that you think "shouldn't" happen, you have the opportunity to go into resistance or surrender to what IS and reach for an expanded perception. As evolving humans, we have the chance to master ourselves and receive the grace of the Great Mystery, that which is beyond our control.

The thought that you create your own reality is a very empowered position in life that reminds you to look inside, take full responsibility, and stop giving away your power by assuming any kind of victim role. It seems more accurate to say that we co-create reality, because all beings, the collective consciousness, our ancestral input, and all manner of subliminal messages are contributing to the "reality" we are "creating." A burning question for me right now is how much can I affect the world I see and experience by expanding my perception and scope of responsibility?

My current understanding is that the mind is divided into conscious, subconscious, and unconscious realms. You may not know how or why you created something, but as soon as you consider that you at least have a part to play in every creation in life, suddenly it dawns on you that you may make a great difference in your own life and in the lives of everyone you touch.

Making conscious what is unconscious is a very worthwhile activity. It doesn't have to involve years of therapy either. In fact, there are ways in which things can be revealed even through play. Suspend disbelief and start looking within to discover the conditioned habits of thinking and responses to life. This path will offer a lot more freedom and lightness in life. Maybe things really aren't the way you've always assumed they were. Maybe, just maybe, things could be as different as you could imagine them to be.

Most everyone has been programmed by their schooling to value their mind over their heart or senses. This is the masculine, left-brain aspect; while the heart, the feeling nature, the sensual and creative natures are the right-brain, feminine attributes.

What you want is to bring balance within so that both of these are fully functioning as you approach all of the situations and circumstances that arise in life.

Emotional equanimity = not getting triggered + higher frequency vibration = a more graceful and compassionate choice or response than the unconscious, automatic reaction that can leave you feeling discouraged and judging yourself or others.

There are some great resources for clearing subconscious programming. One is Emotional Freedom Technique, another is called The Emotion Code. There are also Transformational Breathwork, The Gene Keys, Non-Violent Communication, and Access Consciousness among many many others.

Emotional Freedom Technique (EFT)

Emotional Freedom Technique (EFT), also known as Meridian Tapping, is a simple and remarkably effective technique for raising awareness of what you're feeling, bringing it more fully into consciousness, then tapping on certain points along the meridians (energy flows in the body) to release them. This technique is always available and works quickly if remembered and used whenever emotions arise.

When feeling an emotion or experiencing any kind of thought of lack, physical challenge, financial challenge, or just raw emotion, identify it and bring it to the surface of your conscious awareness. Inquire within as to the intensity of the feeling. Give it a number between 1 and 10, 10 being the most intense. Then set yourself up to clear this feeling by saying: "Even though I'm feeling ______(whatever you're feeling), I deeply and completely love and accept myself." Repeat this "set up" statement three times while tapping on the "karate chop points" on the outside of the hand or while massaging the lymphatic drainage points on the chest. The lymphatic drainage points are in an indented place between the ribs on the upper chest, straight up from your nipples. They're usually somewhat sore.

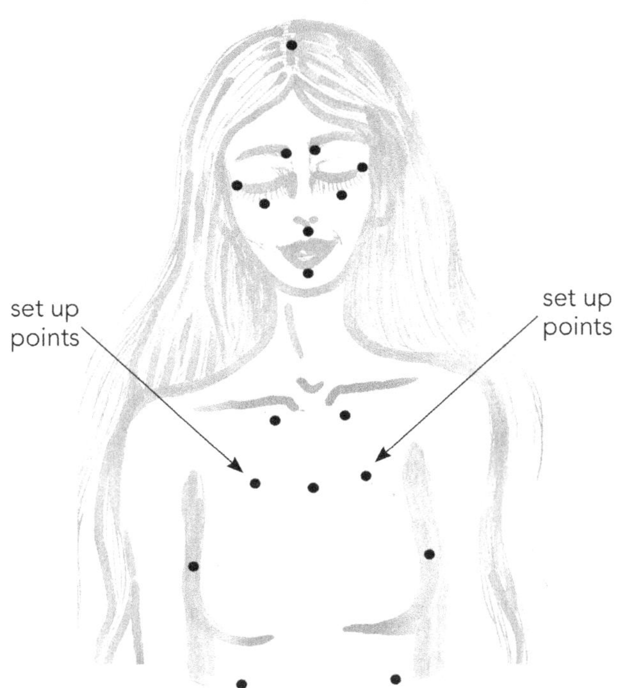

One essential thing that happens when you make the above statement is that you are already identified with another aspect of yourself who is actually witnessing the feeling rather than being consumed by it. THIS IS VERY POWERFUL IN ITS OWN RIGHT. You can be consumed by an emotion, or you can ascend to a vantage point within yourself where you can have compassion for that aspect of yourself that is feeling the feeling.

While stating the feeling, tap on the following sequence of points (see chart above for specific locations), when the points are on both sides of the body, you can tap on either point or on both points at once:

- Inner eyebrow
- Outer edge of the eye socket

- Directly under the eye on the cheek bone
- Under the nose
- Chin point (in the cleft)
- Just under the collar bones
- Under the arm (at about mid bra strap level)
- Under the nipple (on ribs)
- Top of the head
- Heart Center

(While the heart center point is not one of the standard EFT points, one of my early mentors in this process used it, and it really opened the floodgates for me.)

Repeat the sequence until the energy shifts. It is not recommended that you stay with the original emotion but follow the flow of emotions or realizations of the deeper aspects or causes. At some point in the process, when you realize the deeper cause, forgiveness might arise, either for yourself, another, or for media or cultural programming.

For example:

"Even though my tooth is hurting right now, I deeply love and accept myself" (say three times while pressing lymph drainage points)

"This painful tooth" (tap inner brow point)

"This painful tooth" (tap side of eye)

"Oh, this painful tooth" (tap under the eyes on cheekbone)

"Releasing the pain I feel in my tooth" (tap under nose)

"Releasing this pain from my energy system" (tap cleft of chin)

"I am willing to let go of this tooth pain" (tap under collar bones)

"I'm feeling sorrow that I didn't take better care of my teeth" (tap under arm)

"I even feel a little guilt about this" (tap under nipple)

"I really regret that it's come to this" (tap top of head)

"I forgive my earlier self for neglecting to care for my teeth better" (tap heart center)

I might notice a small shift with this sequence. I check in. What is the number I would give to the intensity of this feeling now? It's definitely less, but I want to keep going. As I prepare for round two, I realize that other underlying feelings in this scenario are sorrow, guilt, regret, and shame. So, in the next round I will tap on these emotions, starting with the emotion that seems to have the most charge and go with it, seeing where it leads. I have witnessed rapid results both emotionally and physically using meridian tapping. There are many resources about this technique all over the internet.

The Emotion Code

The Emotion Code was brought in by Dr. Bradley Nelson. He wrote a book, *The Emotion Code*, and teaches workshops describing and demonstrating a process of using muscle testing to discover hidden or trapped emotions, bringing them into conscious awareness and then releasing them. He uses magnets to clear these emotions from the governing channel of the body or the location where they are held. I have had a lot of fun with this technique and also have been able to bring into awareness some amazing insights and stories which led to powerful emotional releases. I have also discovered that I AM a magnet, and I don't necessarily need to use magnets for the clearing. One powerful thing that he teaches is that we are most successful when we invoke the energy of love and gratitude both for the person who is clearing and also for the process we are using. These two energies, love and gratitude, raise vibrational frequency in any situation.

If you find you are comfortable with muscle testing, this is a great technique. One of the most powerful processes he describes is that of discovering and dismantling the "heart wall." Through practicing this technique, I have discovered that most people have an energetic wall built around their heart that is composed of a series of unprocessed emotions. The heart wall serves the person by protecting them from deeply feeling painful emotions. However, it also insulates them from feeling the full spectrum of feelings including joy, happiness, freedom, bliss. Clearing the heart wall is a process that happens over some time. Some people even "need" to maintain some protection over their heart, but it can go from being a rock wall to being a gossamer veil ... easily moved aside.

Transformational Breathwork

Transformational Breathwork is a process of consciously using the breath to free the diaphragm, which is contracted during times of stress and often not fully released. Using conscious connected breathing, or circular breathing, where there is no pause between the inhale and the exhale, is common to many of the most well-known types of transformational breathwork. Conscious connected breathing increases the vibrational frequency and oxygenates the blood. On a deeper level, it can bring up some powerful emotional releases.

Here are a few different types of breathwork you could explore if this type of modality calls to you:

- Breath Mastery created by Dan Brule
- Holotropic Breathing created by Stanislav Grof
- Rebirthing Breathwork created by Leonard Orr
- The Presence Process developed by Michael Brown

Access Consciousness

"Whatever point of view we have, the universe will prove us right because the universe loves us that much." Rikka Zimmerman

Access Consciousness is a body of work developed by Gary Douglas, and it is taught by many teachers. One very vivacious teacher of this work is Rikka Zimmerman.

There are several different aspects to the Access Consciousness work. It is a process of recognizing our unlimited nature as consciousness and witnessing, questioning, and dissolving limiting patterns of thinking and belief, then directing affirming statements in the most expansive and life-affirming ways possible while moving energy through the body.

If this calls to you, please look for resources online.

Non-Violent Communication (NVC)

Non-violent communication was developed by Marshall Rosenberg.

In NVC you identify 4 things:

- What you are feeling
- What the feeling triggers in you (a memory of feeling this way in the past or this pattern)
- Your underlying need
- A request

Engaging in the practice of NVC gives you an opportunity to witness yourself again and in the midst of (perhaps) some intense feeling states. It provides a pause to reflect, look deeper, and turn inward to discover something helpful and bridging rather than something reactive and divisive.

Many of the ways you feel were learned early in life by experiences you had as a child, and if you wake up and become conscious in the midst of the feeling, you can move beyond automated responses. NVC is very powerful work. It's also about taking full responsibility. It's never about, "I feel this because YOU..." but turning that statement around and saying instead, "I feel this because I ...," which allows you to claim your power in a very real way. You can never change "others," but you can change your own reactions and cultivate compassion for yourself by shedding light on why you feel the ways you do and what the underlying precious need is.

The Gene Keys

The Gene Keys, by Richard Rudd, is a beautiful book that identifies certain traits based on your astrology and human design. Then it maps an evolutionary journey from the shadow aspect of that trait to the gift, to the siddhi, the enlightened way that particular trait manifests for you. If this sounds interesting, read the introduction online, and if it resonates with you, get the book and study it. It is a wonderful journey of discovery about your personal potential and our collective evolutionary potential.

Taking time to become soft and open in the realms of the heart in order to allow any unprocessed or unconscious emotions to arise and be witnessed and released is of vital importance not only for an individual, but also for the whole of humanity. Remember that all of us interface with the unified field, where everything and everyone is connected. By raising your own vibrational frequency, you contribute to a field where that connection is more easily accessed by all. You can turn from a reactive state of fear to a conscious choice for Love and Unity over and over again.

CHAPTER ELEVEN

Working with Your Mind

Ayurveda was said to have emerged to promote health and longevity so that one could pursue their spiritual journey without distraction from the body, mind, or emotional imbalances.

Interestingly, many of the yogic practices, which are thousands of years old, are in complete alignment with quantum theory. Simply stated, we affect the quantum field (the field of all possibilities) with our own inner state. This inner state is a combination of thoughts and behaviors that inspires feeling states.

Even though many people now believe that the way they think has some effect on their lives, most of us do not regularly engage in conscious practices to literally create the future.

Without meaning to sound boastful, I will share with you that I am living the life of my (waking) dreams, literally. For many years I have envisioned a beautiful, land-based healing community near water. A place where people could come to re-member their own true nature and their connection with the natural world. A place that, by simply existing, could inspire people to actually change the way they live. I now find myself in such a place, and it is even better than I imagined!

After 20 plus years on this path (and definitely NOT following it as well as I could have, STILL!), I feel better than ever in my body and being. I awake daily, pain free and inspired, feeling light, healthy, motivated, and happy. It is very rare that I ever get "sick." I am in love with life!

I am consciously perpetuating this dream by being in gratitude and giving thanks many times per day for how life has choreographed these exact circumstances I have dreamed of and for the people who join in them. Together, we have co-created this magnificent rendezvous!

I invite you to take some time each day in the most sacred spot in the universe, your own heart. If you haven't already, start "painting" a picture in your mind of your dream life, whatever that is! And then, feel into it in your imagination. Where are you? Who is with you? What is your state of health? Add as much detail as you can. Are there birds singing? Flowers? Water? And the most important piece, how do you feel in this life? Are you deeply at peace? Content? Ecstatic? Joyful? Are you living your purpose? Are you fulfilled?

If you haven't thought it possible to have anything more or different than what you have now, you haven't really tapped the power of the universe, the power that lives through you. Start now. Remember that your mind and body are one. True health starts in the mind. I truly believe that everyone has access to the Divine Intelligence, which magically choreographs meetings and opportunities that we have, somehow, at some time, set in motion ourselves.

I AM perpetuating the dream that humanity will walk on the Earth with reverence as the Spiritual Beings we truly are. I am dreaming that Love will direct our thoughts, our words, and therefore, our actions. I pray that we will all come to realize that we are meant to live in JOY!

Now let's go a little bit more deeply into some Ayurvedic teachings as they relate to your mind. In addition to the three doshas (vata, pitta, kapha), there are three qualities of the mind. They are known as the three gunas. Guna means quality. But they also distinguish patterns of thinking and behavior. The three gunas are called sattva, rajas, and tamas.

QUALITIES OF THE MIND ~ GUNAS

Sattva ~ Harmony and Balance

Sattva is pure thoughts and actions that are peaceful, kind, generous, and stable. A sattvic person knows that the outer circumstances in life are a reflection of their own state of mind. Therefore, they tend to their inner world in a consistent way. A predominantly sattvic person radiates happiness, love, and contentment. We all need more sattva! And, most "spiritual" practices aim at creating techniques to cultivate a sattvic state of mind in order to meet all of life's circumstances with calm equanimity.

Here are ways the sattva guna can express through each type:

- **Vata Sattvic** – Open, creative, expansive, inspired, psychic, artistic, sensitive, joyful
- **Pitta Sattvic** – Clear, focused, powerful, guided, directed, determined, very perceptive
- **Kapha Sattvic** – Unconditional love, generous, compassionate, patient, grounded, stable

Rajas ~ Action and Movement

Rajas is movement or disturbance. It is also the power of transformation, which involves some kind of shift or movement. A rajasic person is more outwardly focused. Rajas is also the vital energy that helps us achieve our goals in life. Rajasic energy can shift both sattvic and tamasic states. It is the dynamic energy that moves and changes things.

Here are ways rajas guna can express through each type:

- **Vata Rajasic** – Ungrounded, overwhelmed, over busy, anxious, nervous, flighty

- **Pitta Rajasic** – Driven, perfectionist, judgmental, angry, controlling, jealous, obsessive
- **Kapha Rajasic** – Stubborn, attached, possessive, complacent

Tamas ~ Inertia

Tamas is the quality of inactivity or stasis. It, too, has its natural place, deep rest being a prime example. But tamas also describes states of mind that are stuck in darkness and ignorance. Tamasic people tend to be closed-minded and lacking awareness. Tamas can also refer to decay, like dead or old food. The focus of tamasic energy is downward. Other tamasic qualities include fear, dullness, and lethargy.

Here are ways tamas guna can express through each type:

- **Vata Tamasic** – Tragically dramatic, depressed, addicted, suicidal
- **Pitta Tamasic** – Violent, psychotic, hateful, vindictive
- **Kapha Tamasic** – Lethargic, hoarding, stealing, extremely attached to things and comfort

Become aware of where your energy is right now. What are the patterns of thinking that define your state of mind? Take an honest look. Once you are aware, it is possible and desirable to consciously cultivate more and more sattvic qualities. Each of the energies has their optimal function: We need rajas to move energy and we need tamas for periods of deep rest or grief, but a general sattvic state is the optimal state of being. From here, we can witness all that life brings to us and have the clarity to meet life in the best possible way.

Spiritual practices like meditation, breath practices (pranayam), mantra practice (chanting sacred phrases) yoga, prayer, affirmation, and visualization actually change the brain and the genes. In fact, your brain is in a state of constant change with every bit of information it receives through your senses, your mind, and your emotions.

By engaging in spiritual practice, you can forge new pathways in your brain. The converse is also true. If you get stuck in ways of thinking and feeling that are less than supportive and life affirming, those pathways are perpetuated throughout your physiology. The more those same pathways are traversed through repetition, the more deep-seated habits are formed. Your life will change to reflect the pathways you create in your brain. The ability for the brain to forge new pathways and actually change learned patterns of thinking and responding is called neuroplasticity. Because of neuroplasticity, the brain's ever-changing potential, anything is possible! You have the capacity to transform your life by affirming new attitudes and actions that forge new pathways in your brain.

Here are some strategies for working with patterns or habits that no longer serve you:

First, identify a pattern or habit that you wish to change. Observe how it is affecting your life and the consequences it has for you. Simply witness the feelings and thoughts you have around it and how it feels in your body. Next, state your intention to change the pattern or habit of ______. Intention is a very powerful way of directing your focus and communicating with your higher self.

Now consciously shift your focus in the direction of what you want instead of what you don't want. Stop giving attention to the unwanted pattern and move towards what you want instead. Notice how this feels in your body. Use your imagination in as much vivid detail as you can to imagine yourself in the new state of freedom you want to create. Practice this often. Repetition is what builds the new pathways in your brain.

Whenever you find yourself thinking in the old way or moving towards the old habit, catch yourself and say, "I don't have to do that anymore. I choose ______ instead." Choose ways of being or things to do instead of following the unwanted habit. Perhaps you want to decide to take a walk rather than eat that, or smoke that, or do that.... Make a decision about it...over and over again until it becomes your reality. Use affirmations or EFT tapping to anchor this new desire.

Listen to the quiet voices inside. Always choose to give attention and power to the ones that make you feel empowered and free, rather than the ones that stimulate guilt. Some people have an unconscious addiction to guilt, which can stem from deep feelings of unworthiness or powerlessness. The more you make choices based on what inspires you to feel genuinely good, the more your own self-esteem will grow. You will gain power and motivation with every small (or big) success.

Through practice, you will become an empowered, light-filled, and loving being. There are very few things you can control in this life, but your own thoughts, habits, and beliefs are things you CAN control.

You can also choose the tools you wish to use. Here are a few reminders for you:

MEDITATION

I like to define meditation as a simple practice of turning your attention inward and directing your attention in some way that suspends the endless mind talk, and in a great session, you get to drop into that silence between the thoughts. That depth of stillness that resides in the throne of your own heart. That field of all possibilities.

- You can meditate on the breath moving in and out of your nose.
- You can meditate by repeating a mantra (a sacred phrase, in Sanskrit or any other language).
- You can meditate on a mandala or yantra (a sacred geometric symbol).
- You can meditate on a candle flame.
- You can meditate by relaxing each muscle in your body one by one.

- You can meditate by focusing your attention on one of your chakras (energy centers of the body).
- You can meditate with a visualization.
- You can even meditate while gardening, cleaning your home, or cooking a meal!

Here is my favorite meditation practice in case you don't have one or want to try something different:

- Sit yourself down and take some time to get very comfortable. Preferably with your spine straight. You can sit in a chair or in a cross-legged posture on the ground or floor. Use a cushion to elevate your hips for more comfort on your knees and low back.
- Now just bring your full attention into your body right where it sits.
- Feel where you touch the surface beneath you.
- Feel your clothing against your skin.
- Feel any air that is moving across your skin.
- Stay attentive to the feeling of your body, open your sense of hearing, and listen for all the sounds that are available in your space.
- See if you can reach past the sounds to the backdrop of silence behind the sounds.
- Without focusing on anything in particular, just take in the play of color and light in the space you're in.
- Notice any aromas in your space.
- Notice if there is any taste in your mouth.
- Now bring your awareness to your thoughts. Without judgment, just notice what thoughts roll by, don't attach to any of them, but let them move like clouds across the sky.

- Finally, notice any feelings you may be experiencing. This could be an emotion or a feeling in the body.
- Now ... turn your attention toward the one who is noticing.
- Who or what is that Presence, that silent witness?
- You are not your body, your senses, your thoughts, or your feelings ... because you can witness all of those. YOU ARE THE WITNESS, THE EXPERIENCER, THE SOURCE AND CENTER OF YOUR OWN UNIVERSE!

BREATH

Let's explore the breath. There are many ways to use your breath to clear your mind and energize your whole being. Breath practice is a magical doorway to open you up to things you may not have even known were there. Breath can help release emotional energy. Breath can help you be with pain, emotional or physical.

Breathing is the only system in the body that is completely under your control and also completely involuntary. With every breath you receive, you are not simply breathing in the air, you are breathing in life force energy. You are breathing in love. And with each exhale, you release not only carbon dioxide, but you can release stress, tension, anxiety, pain. Breathing also massages all of your internal organs.

You can have a love affair with every breath! Breath is the first gift you receive in this life, and it is freely given all throughout your life. Come to appreciate breath as the precious gift it is. For truly, without it, your body will die. So, breathe in a way that energizes your body and soothes your soul. Find pleasure in the simple act of breathing. Use your breath to get out of your head and into your body.

I've heard it said that the longest journey you must take is the journey from your head to your heart. When you breathe consciously into and out of your heart, you are able to receive so much love from the universe and also send out love to all that is. And the truth is that breath itself is breathing you. The spirit of life breathes you. I believe it is no accident that breathing is taking place right around your heart. As you use your breath to open and expand, to let go and relax, you are activating your heart center. When you change the way you breathe, you can change the way you feel. You can also improve the functioning of your body with conscious breathing.

If you stand barefoot on the ground and become conscious of your breathing with an intention to connect to the Earth, you'll begin to feel that connection. Here is a very simple breathing meditation you can do: Breathing in, draw energy up from the Earth through your feet, your legs, and up into your body; and then, relaxing, send that breath down through your body and back into the Earth. This is a powerful practice because when you ground with the Earth, you start to resonate at the same frequency as the Earth. Then the Earth itself is more of a support for you.

You are a bridge between the spiritual and the material. Who you are, the truth of your being is always here—pure, silent, and still—regardless of what comes and goes or what happens in your life. Use your breath to begin to touch this place in you, and practice conscious breathing throughout the day to forge a clear pathway to that stillness.

If you find yourself lying awake at night, unable to sleep, rather than regretting being awake, try thinking wonderful thoughts. Breathe beautiful comfortable breaths, and make use of that time to love yourself and to deeply relax your body.

Often if you wake at night, it's difficult to let go into sleep again because your mind is busy. Breathing is a simple way to quiet your mind. Rather than resisting being awake, simply breathe in and breathe out; try taking a breath for 4 counts, hold it in for 4 counts, then release for 4 counts; repeat this pattern and soon you may surrender into sleep.

Experiment with each of the following pranayam (conscious breathing) practices. Notice how you oxygenate your whole body when you practice kapalabhati. Notice the quality of silent awareness that comes about when you practice ujjayi breathing. And notice how focused your mind becomes when you practice alternate nostril breathing.

A Simple Yogic Cleansing Breath – Inhale slowly, and completely fill your belly, ribs, and chest; then slowly exhale, starting with your chest, then your ribs, and finally your belly.

Alternate Nostril Breathing (Nadi Shodhana) – To still and focus your mind. Nadi Shodhana is balancing for all three doshas. Use your thumb and fourth finger to close off the nostril you are not breathing through, and proceed like this:

- Inhale deeply
- Cover right, breathe out left
- Cover left, breathe in right
- Keep left covered, breathe out right
- Cover right, breathe in left

This is 1 round. Start with 5 rounds and work your way up to 12 rounds. Simply keeping track of what you're doing keeps the mind very focused. You will notice a sense of heightened clarity and calm after this practice.

Ujjayi Breath (Ocean breath) – Slightly close the back of your throat so you can hear your breath when you inhale. When you've got it, inhale for 5-8 counts, hold for 2-4 counts, and exhale out for 5-8 counts (play with increasing number of counts).

Try walking with ujjayi breath, taking 20 steps during 1 inhale and exhale cycle. Or try this if you wake at night. Works like a dream. Ujjayi breath decreases vata dosha.

Bhastrika (Bellows breath) – Rapid active exhale contracting tummy muscles followed by an equally rapid inhale. Bhastrika increases pitta and agni for better digestion.

Kapalabhati (Skull Shining) – A cleansing breath where you forcefully exhale while contracting your tummy muscles, then passively allow the breath to fill the space when you relax your tummy.

There are so many more ways to work with your mind. Start with an intention to do so, and see what comes into your experience. Perhaps it's some solitary time in nature, perhaps a long swim. Try different ways of directing your attention, even if it's just being totally present in your hands when you wash dishes. Anything and everything you do or choose not to do can be practices to rein in the mind and experience a deeper state of being.

CHAPTER TWELVE

Week One ~ Purvakarma Preparing the Body and Mind for Cleansing

OK, here we go! In this section, I will list all of the things you need to do during week one of this cleanse. I will elaborate on each suggestion below, then provide you with a checklist at the end of this chapter for quick reference. This list will also be in Chapter 17, titled "Cleanse at a Glance," on page 175.

Timing is everything!

You want to plan to start this cleanse so that on days five and six you can have rest days, where you have nothing else you need to do. This phase of preparation is setting you up to do a purge that may interrupt your normal sleep pattern on the night of day five, so you will want to have an open day for rest the following day.

Set up a sacred space.

To allow for the mind to relax and to really be able to get the most out of this practice, clearing your space will really help. You do not want to be distracted by things that really need to be done. You will want to share with your family and friends what you are doing and ask them to give you some space to focus on yourself during this time.

Create a comfortable and private place to do your daily self-massage and meditation. If you have a spacious bathroom, that would be perfect; if not, a corner of your bedroom or living room will do fine. Lay down a sheet or towel that you don't mind sacrificing; you may get the oil out of it but maybe not. If you want, you can lay it down over a yoga mat to make a softer place for your daily rituals.

Get yourself a vase of flowers, find a beautiful candle, and/or set out crystals, sacred stones, feathers, or other objects that remind you of the beauty of life. You could make a small altar to focalize your energy during the cleanse. If you have a beloved who inspires you, a teacher, friend, spouse, or children, you may want to include a photo of them.

Identify and write out an intention for your cleanse.

Having an intention for your cleanse will give you a focus for this time. Your intention can be anything. Stating your intention gives it power. You may also want to have a journal just for your PK experiences. It can be very helpful to write down what comes up for you and do some intentional processing. As you look back on this cleansing time, you will see and be able to celebrate breakthrough moments and those "aha's!"

Be in silence, reflecting inwardly as much as you can.

Read or tune into your intentions often.

Rest as much as possible. This is really important! You are doing a cleanse. You can expect to feel extra tired or heavy as toxins are being mobilized. Especially by the end of this first week when you are eating a large amount of ghee in the morning, you may feel nauseous, heavy, or lethargic. Honor your body and rest. This too shall pass!

Be silent unless you really need to speak. You lose a lot of energy talk talk talking all of the time. If you must continue to work or engage in your family life, take what time you can, even if it's 15 minutes to simply be quiet, breathe, meditate, and contemplate how you are living your life and where you want to go. Even if you do this while you are massaging oil onto your skin ... take time to settle your mind.

Eat a mono diet of kitchari as much as you're able to.

Eat kitchari or a clean whole food fat-free diet favoring vegetable soups and stews. Recipe for kitchari is in Chapter 15 on page 136.

During this cleanse, it is traditional to eat kitchari for every meal. Once you learn how to make it, it's really very delicious and satisfying. Going on a mono-diet for a period of time helps quiet your mind and gives your digestive system a rest. Kitchari is considered the supreme healing food in Ayurveda. I have heard that the word kitchari is sometimes translated as "Food of the Gods."

For most people, kitchari is very easy to digest. It is a complete protein with the combination of legumes, grains, digestive spices, and vegetables. The vegetables and grains provide fiber that scrub the colon. The legumes are astringent and therefore have a pulling action to draw dislodged toxins out. The spices in the kitchari are all digestive aids and balance the digestive fire as well as stimulate the liver to detoxify. If you cannot eat kitchari for any reason, relax. Eat warm soups and steamed veggies; just eat simply, and practice mindful eating.

Avoid eating any other fats this first week, especially as you are specifically targeting your fat cells during this cleanse. When you have the ghee (or other oil) in the mornings, you are stimulating fat metabolism. You want your body to process the accumulations in your own fat cells rather than any fat you eat, so avoid eating any! If you need help with this, refer to the Ama Reducing Diet in chapter 15.

Eat Beet Apple Cilantro Salad frequently.

See Chapter 15, page 151 for recipe.

This salad is designed to assist your cleansing process. The beets help to thin the bile so that it can break down fatty or mucus-y accumulations in the villi in the intestines. When the digestion is sluggish or overwhelmed, these villi can get overloaded and gunked up with mucus. What has caused this mucus to form? UNDIGESTED AND UNASSIMILATED FOOD OR EXPERIENCES (information that we have received through the senses) that the body stores in fat cells. A buildup of sticky mucus reduces the capacity of the colon to digest and assimilate; then waste materials back up into the liver for another round of processing, which impedes the natural flow of healthy digestion.

The apples aid in softening any stones that may be in the liver or gall bladder. The cilantro is specific for binding to metals that are being released during the cleanse. The ginger and lemon or lime add to the alkalizing effect as well as stimulate metabolism.

Drink blood cleansing teas, 2-3 cups each day.

Some good teas for detoxifying the blood are dandelion root, burdock root, red clover blossom, ginger, turmeric, and licorice root. If you feel confident and adventurous, try making your own blood cleansing tea with whole, organic herbs. Otherwise, at any store that carries natural foods, you should be able to get a Detox Tea and/or Roasted Dandelion Root Tea. Be sure you do not get any tea that has laxatives in it, especially senna, which is very aggravating to the digestive system and should only be taken in an emergency situation, one time. You can develop a dependency on laxatives, which will weaken your body's own elimination capabilities.

Take ½ tsp. of triphala powder in ½ cup warm water before bed.

Blood cleansing tablets (by Banyan Botanicals) are a perfect compliment to this cleanse. Take 4 per day.

A great combination of herbs to balance the digestive fire (samana vayu) is cumin seed, coriander seed, and fennel seed made into a tea, ½ tsp. each in 1 quart of water. Bring to boil, then simmer for 15 minutes. Enjoy throughout your day.

Ginger tea taken before a meal is also very beneficial for enkindling the agni.

Sip hot water throughout the day every 10-15 mins.

When hot water is taken in this way, it doesn't simply go to the bladder. You'll find that you are actually absorbing the water and rehydrating the cells instead.

Morning oil pulling.

Oil pulling should be done as soon as you get out of bed. Go ahead and look at your tongue first and use a tongue scraper or a spoon to clean your tongue. Then, put 1 tsp. of either raw, organic sesame or coconut oil in your mouth and swish it around and through your teeth for 15-20 minutes. You will notice it changing color and texture. Spit it out into the toilet or outside and then brush your teeth really well, floss, and scrape your tongue again.

Internal oleation: ingesting increasing amounts of oil each morning.

Taking ghee each morning on an empty stomach for 4-6 days is key to this cleanse. Besides the benefit of stimulating fat metabolism as explained previously, the oils are being absorbed into the tissues, lubricating them, and dissolving fat, like using soap on an oily pan. This step is the key difference between this cleanse and other types of cleansing regimens. Ingesting oil specifically targets fat-soluble toxins which could have been stored in your system for years. If you have high cholesterol or another reason you don't want to eat ghee, you can use another high quality oil: flax, hemp, sesame, or coconut are all outstanding oils.

For some people, it is simple to take the ghee; for others, it's more difficult. Try melting it and taking it either on a spoon or just drinking it down. When the amounts get larger, you may need to take 2 tsp. at a time with a pause in between doses. Follow your ghee with a cup of hot ginger tea, which will help disperse the oil and ease any sense of nausea that you may experience.

You can also put the ghee right into your tea and drink it down that way. Or add a squeeze of lemon or lime to the ghee.

A modest oleation schedule is as follows:

Day 1 - 1 tsp. (Measured teaspoon)
Day 2 - 2 tsp.
Day 3 - 3 tsp.
Day 4 - 4 tsp.
Day 5 - 6 tsp.

If you are strong and have robust digestion, you may convert teaspoons to tablespoons. Many people do.

Your stools may look oily by day five. Your skin may also be glowing with oil. You may even smell like ghee! One key to knowing when you've had enough is that you will feel an acute aversion to taking any more ghee! This is totally normal and expected and different for everyone.

You will purge and cleanse the small intestine, liver, and gall bladder the night following your last morning dose of oil. See instructions for virechana on page 112.

Massage warmed oil into your skin daily, followed by a hot bath or shower.

Oiling your body both internally and externally is called snehana in Ayurveda. Snehana or snehan translates to love. Along with the internal oiling, a daily oil massage is the other very important aspect of this method. You will be massaging warm oils into your skin daily, which will saturate your tissues from the outside. Since the oil is warm, it opens the pores and starts loosening stored toxins. Also, loving yourself in this way sends a flood of healing chemicals to your skin and all throughout your nervous system. This is a clear message of love, honor, and appreciation for your body. You are also increasing circulation, stimulating the lymph, lubricating the subtle channels of the body (called nadis), and softening and deeply cleansing the skin.

If you can and you are inclined to, you can leave it on while doing some yoga or gentle stretching and movement. Then, after 20 minutes or so take either a steam bath, a hot bath, or a shower without soap. This will further open the tissues and subtle channels of your body so that stored accumulations can easily move out from where they have been and into the organs of elimination for release. If you are able to, wrap up in a sheet and warm blanket or sleeping bag and break a sweat.

If all you can do is a five-minute oiling before or even after a hot shower, then that's all you can do, and that's just fine. But, if you can spend some extra time focusing your appreciation on your body while oiling it, that will be beneficial to you. Any time you can spend on the oil massage is good. Here is an anointing ritual you can try, to acknowledge your body.

Self-anointing ritual.

Warm about half a cup of high quality organic oil. Almond, coconut, sunflower, or sesame are a few good options. Create a safe and comfortable place to BE with yourself for as long as it takes to enact this ritual, 15 minutes or so. Perhaps light a candle and remember your intention.

As you minister to yourself, feel an upwelling of appreciation for each part of your body and how it serves you, so often without thought or recognition. Gently apply some warm oil to each part of your body as you acknowledge, thank, and honor it. Conjuring up a state of Love and Gratitude uplifts your vibrational frequency, which changes everything.

Enjoy every moment.

As you massage yourself, you can say:

I become conscious of my body as a temple, and I honor each aspect fully and with great gratitude.
The crown of my head is the opening for my spirit.
My face is the vehicle of expressing my heart.
My ears receive the vibrations of sound and enrich my world.
My eyes are windows for my spirit.
My mouth allows me to communicate, smile, and kiss.
My teeth help me to receive the nourishment of food.
My nose allows me to smell.
I celebrate my neck, which supports my head and helps me to turn and shift my focus.
My arms and hands allow me to touch, caress, and soothe myself and others.
My heart and chest are the altar of my body temple.
My lungs open to receive the breath of life effortlessly.
My breasts are beautiful and nourishing.
My ribs create a protected place for my organs.
My liver, spleen, pancreas, and intestines serve me so well to digest all I take in and transform it into pure love light.
My belly is where laughter emerges.
My genitals offer me sacred pleasure and profound creativity.
My spine supports my uprightness in the world and allows me flexibility.
My legs allow movement for my spirit.
My feet take me wherever I want to go.
I fully honor my sense of touch.
I fully honor my sense of hearing.
I fully honor my sense of sight.
I fully honor my sense of taste.
I fully honor my sense of smell.
I am grateful to be fully here, now.
I am a vessel for love to pour into the world.
Just as I am!

Week One Overview

- Clear your time and create sacred space for yourself.
- Identify and write out an intention for your cleanse.
- Be in silence, reflecting inwardly as much as you can.
- Eat kitchari as much as you're able to or a clean, whole food, fat-free diet (recipe on page 136).
- Eat Beet Apple Cilantro Salad frequently (recipe on page 151).
- Drink blood cleansing teas, 2-3 cups each day (page 104).
- Sip hot water throughout the day every 10-15 mins.
- Drink lemon water, minimum 1 quart daily.
- Do oil pulling daily (page 105).
- Internal oleation daily for 5 days (page 105).
- Massage warmed oil into your skin daily, followed by a hot bath or shower and wrap (pages 106-107).

Recommended daily routine for week one

- Wake with the sun (around 6:00 AM). Give thanks for the day!
- Empty your bladder and bowels.
- Wash your face and rinse your eyes.
- Warm your daily dose of ghee and take it on an empty stomach.
- Drink a cup of hot ginger tea.
- Clean your teeth and tongue.
- Oil pull.
- Self-anointing (oil massage with warm oil).
- Gentle yoga, pranayam, meditation.

- Sweat therapy: bath or shower, sauna, bio-mat.
- Make your teas for the day.
- Take your blood cleansing tablets.
- Breakfast IF YOU ARE HUNGRY (at least 1 hour after having your ghee, ideally by 8:00 AM).
- Worldly duties (sipping hot water or blood cleansing teas during the day).
- ½ hour before eating lunch, have a thin slice of ginger with a little salt or a cup of ginger tea to increase agni.
- Lunch (between 10:00 AM & 2:00 PM).
- Second work cycle (no drinks for an hour after eating lunch, then resume hot water and/or tea).
- Late afternoon walk in nature or a nap if needed.
- Dinner (between 5:00 & 6:00 PM).
- Wind down for bedtime: meditation, calming yoga, calming pranayam, bath, spiritual reading.
- Bedtime before 10:00 PM.

Avoid strenuous activity, extreme temperatures, and wind. Be gentle; protect and care for yourself like you would a baby.

CHAPTER THIRTEEN

Week Two ~ Panchakarma Main Cleansing Practices

Panchakarma refers to the five purifying processes of this cleanse. First you prepare, then you purify, then you rejuvenate.

By the end of the first week, you may be feeling sluggish, heavy, tired, or slightly nauseous. This is not unusual. You have mobilized a lot of accumulated toxins in your body. Perhaps this has also allowed trapped emotions to rise to the surface. Give thanks that things are moving and changing. This week you will start to purge your system of these accumulations, and you will start to feel lighter and brighter!

You may want some support from a loved one at this point. If you are alarmed in any way by how you are feeling, please check in with an Ayurvedic practitioner or other natural health practitioner for reassurance if you need to.

You will continue with the daily warm oil massage and sweating this week.

Continue with the simple diet of kitchari or soups, along with steamed vegetables and beet salad. Continue taking blood cleansing teas and herbs.

After the five days of the internal snehana (eating increasing amounts of ghee or oil) that happened in the first week, you will be ready for your purge. Ideally, you would be monitored by an Ayurvedic practitioner who could determine the exact best time when you were ready based on changes in your pulse, your skin, digestive signs, emotional changes, etc. But, if you are doing this cleanse on your own, hopefully you will notice when you feel SATURATED. When you are saturated, even the thought of eating any more oil is enough to make you feel nauseous. You may feel heaviness in your belly, your skin may be extra oily, you may see oil in your stools. Even if you don't feel any of these, plan to go ahead and do the purge on day six.

VIRECHANA

The purge of the small intestine (the seat of pitta), liver, and gall bladder is called virechana in Ayurveda. The preparations during the first week were to prepare the body for virechana. You will be working with an awareness of the pitta time of day, between 10:00 AM - 2 :00 PM, and you will be consciously stimulating pitta on your virechana day.

Have all your treatment protocols done before lunch hour. Eat lunch during pitta time of day, as close to noon as possible. Make your food extra spicy and oily for this day. You may want to sauté onions and garlic in ghee or oil, and/or add hot peppers or tomatoes to your kitchari. Onions and garlic are considered "rajasic", and they can stir up the energy in your body and mind, which is totally appropriate for this day. You will be finishing your last meal of the day by 6:30 PM. This is more fully explained below.

After eating lunch, rest a bit, then spend some time focalizing your intention for the purge. What is it you want to release with the purge? Do you have patterns of anger, jealousy, harsh judgments, perfectionism? These are all pitta attributes, and you may ask them to go during your purge.

If you have an appropriate place to do so, go somewhere where you can make a small fire. Even a candle will do. Gaze into the fire while focusing on what you want to release. Write these things down on a piece of paper and burn them up in your fire if it's safe to do so.

Virechana is specific for cleansing pitta from the small intestine, liver, and gall bladder. It also cleanses vata from the colon. This is generally a very easy process, though different for everyone. Some people have many more movements than other people. Get as much rest as you can before, during, and after. You may feel drained the following day, or you may feel great! Relax and allow the process.

Please start your last meal by 6:00 PM and finish by 6:30 PM on the day of your purge. It takes approximately 2.5 hours for your food to enter the small intestine, so 2.5 hours after you finish eating, at 9:00 PM, take 2-3* full Tbsp. of castor oil mixed well in ¼ cup fresh orange juice. Chase with ½ cup plain fresh OJ to cut the taste. Go right to bed after taking the castor oil.

*Note: If you are a very small person, you may take 2 Tbsp. instead of 3. However, even if you are a big person, 3 Tbsp. is usually quite sufficient. It is also possible to take a different laxative instead of the castor oil if you prefer. However, I have witnessed the castor oil work beautifully hundreds of times. The goal is a complete emptying of the intestine.

At some time you will awaken with the urge to empty your bowels. Give yourself plenty of time on the toilet. Drink a cup of water each time you go to the bathroom to keep the process going and avoid dehydration. You should expect several bowel movements over the next few hours. You can go until you are eliminating mostly clear liquid. Your movements may be solid to begin with, then getting lighter and yellow or green near the end. This is a release of bile.

Allow yourself to sleep in the day after the purge. In fact, take the whole day to relax, rest, contemplate, and meditate. Let go of all of your protocols for today.

On this day it is also common to "fast" on liquids to slowly rebuild the digestive fire again. This is called samsarjana krama.

SAMSARJANA KRAMA: Gradually Reintroducing Food

After your virechana, you will need to gradually rebuild your agni (digestive fire) in the following way:

Take ¾ of a cup of white basmati rice (or millet or quinoa if you are wanting or needing to avoid eating grains) and put it in 6 cups of water, bring to a boil, and cook until really soft.

Blend half of the cooked rice, millet, or quinoa in a small amount of the cooking water and a couple of slices of fresh ginger root until creamy. Mix into a larger amount of hot water to make a quart of kanji. Add a pinch of cinnamon, cardamom, and a teaspoon of honey.

Blend the second half of the rice, millet, or quinoa in water to make a second quart of the kanji. Add 2-4 Tbsp. miso*, 3-4 slices fresh ginger root, 2-3 slices fresh turmeric or ½ tsp. powdered turmeric, a ½ tsp. cumin seed or powder, juice of ½ lemon or lime, and a handful of fresh cilantro. Blend again to make a lovely soup.

*Note: Miso is a live food. Do not cook it but add to the water that is already heated and cooled to the point where you can leave your finger in it without burning.

Feeling actual hunger is the signal that your body is ready to digest food. When you feel hungry, sip on these drinks until they are gone. This could take the entire day if your fire is slow to come up or it could happen more quickly. You don't want to add too much food for your system to have to digest after you have effectively put out the digestive fire with your purge.

Think of it as building a fire. First you want to start with kindling, adding small pieces and letting them make the fire hotter before adding any more wood. This is exactly what you're doing today, and it may be helpful to keep this in your consciousness over the next couple of days. What you are doing is consciously rebuilding your digestive fire. Kindling first, then some small pieces of wood; let those burn hot before trying to add a larger piece of wood, which could overwhelm a small fire and just sit and smolder.

These drinks could be your only food for the whole day after your purge. So, while it is a "fasting" day, you will be feeding and stoking your fire. You should use this opportunity to become acutely aware of your body's signals that it is ready for food rather than eating out of habit, conditioned thought, emotional need, or simple desire.

After a day of rest, you will be ready to integrate simple, easy to digest foods into your diet. Perhaps start with a rice and spice soup; the next meal add a steamed vegetable. Then you should be ready to resume your simple diet for the rest of the week.

BASTI TREATMENTS

Next you will address the large intestine with basti treatments. The word basti means bladder, container, or wash. In Ayurveda there are many kinds of bastis: for the eyes, the heart, the sacrum, the vagina, and the colon. There are also many different kinds of bastis for the colon used for different purposes: cleansing, toning, nourishing, lubricating, etc. Basti involves the introduction of liquids, such as herbal decoctions, oils, and even milk, coffee, or bone broth directly into the descending colon.

The basti is so much more comprehensive than an enema! It can be used for many purposes. Basti (referred to here as an enema) is considered the mother of all panchakarma treatments. It cleanses the accumulated ama (toxins) from all the three doshas (vata, pitta, and kapha) through the colon. Basti is also highly beneficial as a rejuvenating treatment. These ministrations are done for a few days, based on your condition. Again, ideally you would consult with an Ayurvedic practitioner to determine the best type of basti or series of bastis for you. Here, I can only speak in universal terms about a very personal practice.

Differing greatly from a simple enema or even a colonic, which only address the eliminative capacity of the colon, basti is said to restore overall balance, especially for a vata type or for vata type imbalances like too much busy-ness, excess thinking, dryness, brittleness, low back pain, difficulty sleeping, and overwhelm. Depending on what substances are used in the basti, it can increase weight in emaciated people or decrease weight in obese people. It can bring back luster, strength, and flexibility to all the tissues of the body, especially the low back, nervous system, reproductive organs, bones, and joints.

The colon is the seat of vata in the body, and vata is the root cause or at least a main factor of many dis-eases. Excess vata lowers overall immune function and speeds up the aging process.

For the basti, you will need an enema bag or enema bucket. These can be found at a good pharmacy or drugstore. If you can't find one where you live, you can order them online. These instructions are for a common enema bag (that often comes as a hot water bottle duo) and a catheter tube.

Ideally, your practitioner will recommend the best type of basti for you. If you don't have an Ayurvedic practitioner available to you and you feel generally strong and confident about doing it, you could make one or more of the following herbal bastis.

To prepare the basti, as a general rule you would bring 3 cups of water to a boil, add herbs, and cook down to 1.5 - 2 cups. This preparation is called a decoction. When the tea has cooled to about body temperature, strain well and add 2 Tbsp. organic cold-pressed sesame oil. Unlike a water enema that is used to flush the colon, the basti is more like an implant that is retained up to 15 minutes (more or less, based on your ability to hold it) and absorbed by the colon.

BASTI RECIPES

- 2 Tbsp. dashmool (or dashamula) root decocted into 2 cups water – cleansing, grounding, tonifying, and warming
- 2 Tbsp. guduchi decocted into 2 cups water – nourishing, building, and warming; however, not aggravating for pitta
- 2 Tbsp. each dashmool & guduchi decocted into in 2 cups water
- 2 Tbsp. ashwagandha root decocted into 2 cups water – nourishing & building, warming
- 2 Tbsp. shatavari root decocted into 2 cups water – nourishing & building, cooling
- 2 Tbsp. brahmi decocted into 2 cups water – calming, soothing, cooling
- 2 Tbsp. amlaki (or amalaki) decocted into 2 cups water – nourishing & cooling
- 1-2 capsules probiotic powder added to 2 cups warm water, ½ cup sesame oil, 2 Tbsp. honey – helps to re-establish intestinal flora, warming and lubricating
- 1 Tbsp. each tonic herbs (ashwagandha, shatavari, amlaki, guduchi) decocted into 1 cup water, then add 1 cup milk – rejuvenating, building, strengthening
- ½ cup ghee – nourishing, lubricating, cooling
- ½ cup organic sesame oil, ¼ cup honey, ½ tsp. (black) salt – nourishing & lubricating, warming

You may mix most of these herbs together for a specific effect as well. You will want to do 1-5 bastis. It is common to start and end with an oil basti.

Coffee Enema: Although not from the Ayurvedic tradition, there are numerous studies on the benefits of doing coffee enemas to detoxify and stimulate your liver. This is a core practice of the Gerson Therapy that has helped thousands heal cancer.

The major benefit of the coffee enema is that it enhances elimination of toxins through the liver. Endoscopic studies confirm it increases bile output. Increased bile flow also alkalinizes the small intestine and promotes improved digestion.

Coffee is bitter & astringent, helping clean the colon walls.

It is said that coffee enemas enhance digestion by increasing bile flow and removing toxins in the large intestine so they will not be reabsorbed. You will need to buy very lightly roasted coffee for this purpose. "Blond Coffee" is said to be the best. Check resources section, starting on page 183, for where to buy.

You use the same method for a coffee enema as for a basti. It is more of a colonic implant than an enema as it is retained in the colon for 15 minutes before expelling.

BASTI INSTRUCTIONS

Warm the basti mixture (tea) until it is a little warmer than body temperature.

Pour well-strained tea into your enema bag.

Open the clip on the hose over a sink until all the air has been forced out of the hose, then close quickly as soon as the liquid starts to come out.

Lubricate the end of the hose with a little oil.

Hang the bag securely above where you will be receiving the basti so the force of gravity will assist in an effortless flow.

Lie on your left side and get comfortable. Insert the basti hose into the rectum, directing it slightly towards the front of the body as you insert it. You will easily be able to go in 4-5 inches before hitting up against the second sphincter that is inside.

Take a breath in and then swallow; as you do, insert the hose past the second sphincter and continue moving it further up past the rectum and into the lower colon until it's about 6-8 inches in. The second sphincter inside your rectum opens up when you swallow. Who knew?

Now, slowly release the hose clip and allow the mixture to enter your colon. If you start to feel pressure, stop and rest for a moment before resuming. Empty the bag entirely and when you're ready, gently remove the hose. Turn onto your right side for a few minutes, then onto your back and rest for 10 - 20 minutes. You may elevate your hips or massage your belly in a clockwise direction while resting. Release into the toilet.

Note: If it's a problem for you to hold the basti, it may be helpful to empty the rectum first, by using some plain warm water that gets expelled preceding your basti.

SHANKA PRAKSHALANA
Five Special Asanas (Poses)

The five asanas which form the core of this particular practice are related directly to the five alimentary valves (sphincters in the digestive tract which act as valves to prevent backflow and control the natural passing through of food.) These asanas help to stretch, massage, tone, and relax all parts of the digestive system & enhance the cleansing process.

The following asanas are used in a yogic cleansing practice for moving energy through the digestive tract. This is usually done while drinking salt water; however I find them beneficial even without. When you try them, you will feel how they massage the belly and the organs. They are a lovely set of asanas to practice while taking yourself through a cleanse. They should be practiced first thing in the morning on an empty stomach or 2 hours after eating. Start slowly, maybe going through the entire sequence 3 times. If that's easy for you, build up to doing the sequence 12 times. ENJOY!

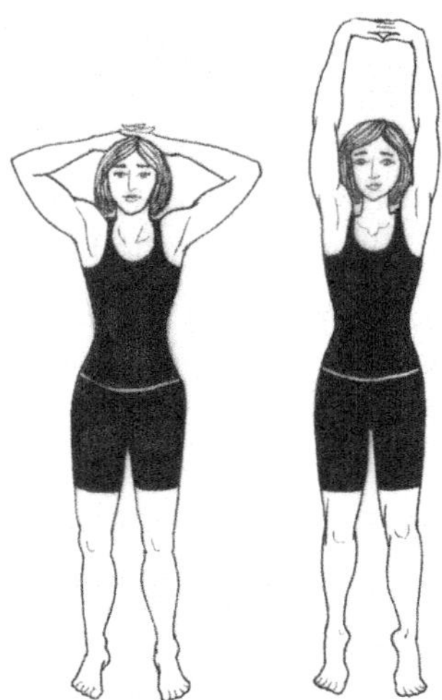

Tadasana - Stretch Pose

Tadasana acts mainly on the stomach and stretches the colon.

- Inhale. Stretch your arms up over your head with your fingers interlocked, palms upward.
- Slowly rise up on your toes, stretching and lengthening your abdominal area.
- Hold the position for a few seconds.
- Exhale, bring your heels down on the floor and hands on top of your head.

Tiryaka Tadasana - Side Bend

Tiryaka Tadasana acts on the small intestine and colon.

- Again, inhale and stretch your arms up over your head with your fingers interlocked, palms upward.
- While exhaling, bend to the right at your waist.
- Hold the position for a few seconds.
- Inhale and slowly come back to standing.
- While exhaling, bend your body to the left side.
- Inhale and slowly come back to standing.

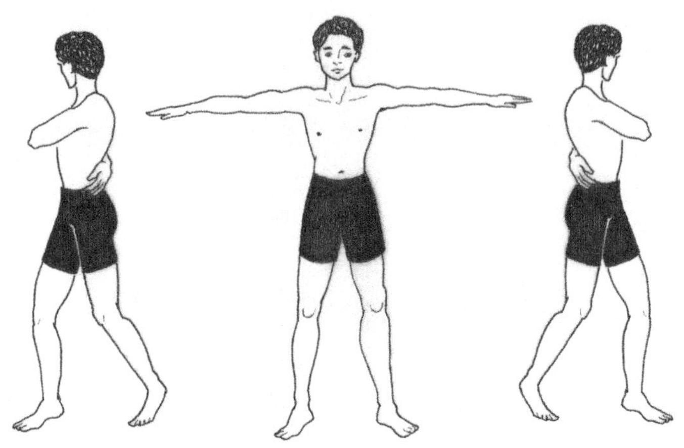

Kati Chakrasana - Twist

Kati Chakrasana massages the small intestine.

- Stand with feet hip distance apart, knees slightly bent and grounded.
- Inhale and then exhale as you twist as far as you can toward the right side.
- Hold this position for a few seconds.
- Inhale and return to the middle.
- Exhale as you twist to the left side.
- Hold this position for a few seconds.
- Inhale and return to center.

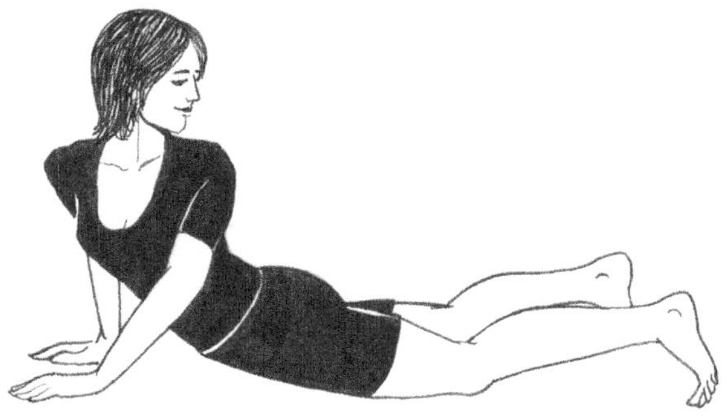

Tiryaka Bhujangasana - Cobra Twist

Tiryaka Bhujangasana squeezes and massages the caecum, sigmoid colon, and rectum and also stimulates the rectal sphincter.

- Lie on the floor with hands directly under your shoulders, forehead touching the floor.
- Now inhale and raise your head up.
- Exhale, twist your head and upper portion of your body to the right side and look over your shoulder, hold for several seconds feeling the diagonal stretch of your belly.
- Inhale and face forward.
- Exhale, twist to the left side, hold for several seconds.
- Inhale and return to the center.

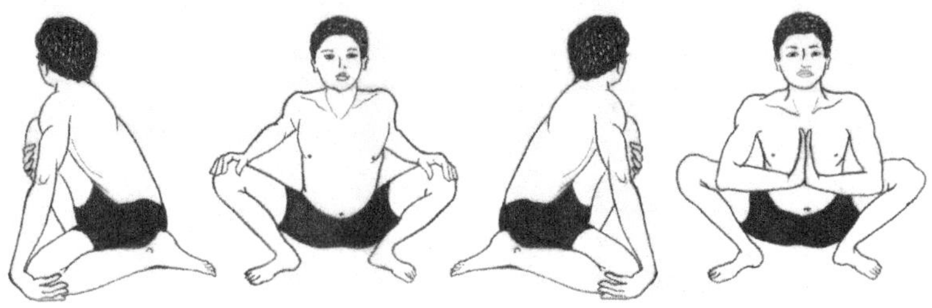

Udarakarshan Kriya - Abdominal Massage Pose

Udarakarshan Kriya squeezes and massages the caecum, sigmoid colon, and rectum and also stimulates the rectal sphincter.

- Come into a squatting position with both hands on your knees, fine for heels to come up if you need to and/or place a rolled blanket under your heels to support your foundation.
- In this squat, take a nice, slow inhale.
- Turn to the right side, exhaling and pushing your left knee to the ground while turning your head to look over your right shoulder.
- Stay here for a few seconds.
- Come back to center on an inhale, bringing your legs back to a squatting position.
- Then, on an exhale, lower your right knee to the floor near your left foot, turning your head to look over your left shoulder.
- Stay here for a few seconds.
- Inhale and come back to center, bringing your legs back to a squatting position; exhale.
- Let your pelvis hang. Bring your palms together in prayer pose.

Week Two Overview

- Do abhyanga (page 55)/swedana (page 56) daily until you complete the virechana and bastis.
- Do virechana (purge) on a day that you can REST THE FOLLOWING DAY (page 112)!
- Samsarjana krama (rebuilding digestive fire) followed by a day of rest (page 114).
- Next, begin bastis, starting and ending with oil basti, doing herbal or coffee basti daily between (pages 115-119).
- Ama-reducing diet (page 71) and blood cleansing teas (page 104).
- Neti (page 76) and/or nasya (page 54), oiling the nostrils daily.
- Do cleansing pranayam daily: bhastrika, kapalabhati, or the simple yogic cleansing breath (pages 98-99).
- Shanka prakshalana asanas daily or some asanas that twist and press your belly (pages 119-124).
- Be in silence as much as you can.
- Rest and reflect on your intention as much as you can.

Recommended daily PK routine for virechana (purge) day

- Wake with the sun (around 6:00 AM). Give thanks for the day!
- Empty your bladder and bowels.
- Wash your face and rinse your eyes.
- Have last dose of ghee.
- Drink a cup of hot ginger tea or warm water.
- Clean your tongue.
- Oil pull.

- Clean your teeth and tongue.
- Self-anointing (abhyanga oil massage with warm oil).
- Nasya (oiling your nostrils).
- Gentle yoga (shanka prakshalana asanas are great today), pranayam, meditation .
- Sweat therapy (swedana) – bath or shower, sauna, bio-mat.
- Breakfast (IF HUNGRY, at least 1 hour after having your ghee, ideally, by 8:00 AM).
- Worldly duties (sipping hot water or blood cleansing teas during the day).
- ½ hour before eating lunch have a thin slice of ginger with a little salt to increase agni.
- Lunch (around noon) Make your food extra oily and spicy today. See recipe for warming kitchari (page 136).
- Second work cycle (no drinks for an hour after eating lunch, then resume hot water and/or tea).
- Late afternoon focused intention ritual or writing.
- Dinner (finish dinner by 6:30 PM) Also warm and spicy.
- At 9:00 PM drink 2-3 Tbsp. of (ideally organic) castor oil.
- Go to bed right away.

Avoid strenuous activity, extreme temperatures, and wind. Be gentle; protect and care for yourself like you would a baby.

Recommended routine for samsarjana krama day

- Allow yourself to sleep in as long as you need after your purge.
- Empty bladder and bowels.
- Wash your face and rinse your eyes.

- Clean your teeth and tongue.
- Drink a glass of warm water.
- Prepare your rice drinks.
- When hungry, sip on rice drinks throughout the day to slowly rebuild agni.
- Rest, reflect, notice how you feel, journal.
- If you need to, because you're very hungry, have a light rice & spice soup.

Recommended daily PK routine for rest of week two

- Wake with the sun (around 6:00 AM). Give thanks for the day!
- Empty your bladder and bowels.
- Wash your face and rinse your eyes.
- Drink a cup of hot ginger tea or warm water.
- Clean your tongue.
- Oil pull.
- Clean your teeth and tongue.
- Self-anointing (oil massage with warm oil).
- Gentle yoga, pranayam, meditation.
- Sweat therapy (swedana) – bath or shower, sauna, bio-mat.
- Take your blood cleansing tablets.
- Breakfast.
- Worldly duties (sipping hot water or blood cleansing teas during the day).
- ½ hour before eating lunch have a thin slice of ginger with a little salt to increase agni.
- Lunch (around noon).

- Second work cycle (no drinks for an hour after eating lunch, then resume hot water and/or tea).
- Late afternoon nap or a walk.
- Dinner (near 6:00 PM).
- Evening basti between 8:30 and 9:00 PM.
- Wind down for bedtime – meditation, calming yoga, calming pranayam, bath, spiritual reading .
- Bedtime before 10:00 PM.

Avoid strenuous activity, extreme temperatures, and wind. Be gentle, protect and care for yourself like you would a baby.

CHAPTER FOURTEEN

Week Three ~ Rasayana Conscious Rejuvenation

Consciously rejuvenating after a cleanse is perhaps the most important and often overlooked step in a complete cleansing practice. This third stage in an Ayurvedic cleanse is called rasayana, which means rejuvenation. Making this time and intention is an act of supreme self-love.

So many who are striving to be their very best are on a perpetual diet or are constantly "cleansing." This is a mistake! A cleanse is an essential cycle that will freshen the tissues for the following cycle, an infusion of nutrients and renewed commitment to practices that will continually enhance your overall health. How long a cycle is, is determined by each individual's condition, strength, and need. For some this is yearly. For others it may be twice a year. And for some it may be at the turn of each season.

Please consult with an Ayurvedic practitioner or doctor to determine if your current condition would benefit from cleansing. In general, everyone can benefit from a cleanse once or twice a year at least. If you have a specific condition, you may benefit from more or less cleansing and more or less building.

Ideally, your daily habits, general diet, and practices (like yoga, meditation, and exercise) should nourish, build, and sustain your strength and vibrancy. Then, a seasonal cleanse will compliment your self-care lifestyle beautifully. Knowing this, consciously going into a phase of replenishing yourself at a really high level following a cleanse will be extremely effective and beneficial. Then, continue to nourish yourself with the self-care practices that follow in the next section.

After a cleanse or a fast, many people want to indulge in the foods that they feel they have been depriving themselves of. If this is sugar, processed foods, or foods that are hard to digest, indulging is not the best choice you can make.

Following panchakarma, all of your tissues are wide open. You have cleansed the deepest channels of your body to allow the free flow of prana, life force. This is a moment of great opportunity! You have a chance now to literally re-make yourself, to take your health and well-being to a whole new level of strength and radiance.

It's been my experience that after panchakarma, if really done thoroughly, people usually have no desire for sugar, chips, bread, or any of their usual "hooks." Instead, they feel a renewed sense of lightness and well-being that inspires them to want to continue living in this way. I know some who have continued to eat kitchari daily well after their cleanse because they felt so much better after their PK. Even when you feel the need for a more diverse menu following panchakarma, please tend to your digestive fire and be gentle with yourself as you come out of cleansing mode.

What you want to do now is consciously build ojas. Food is very important for developing ojas, as ojas is the end product of food. Remember, it takes about a month for the food you eat today to become ojas. Choose the best quality foods you can get ahold of. Eat with conscious awareness, and supplement your good diet and practices with some superfoods and tonics that will help you feel energized and radiant.

Ojas-increasing foods include:

- Dates
- Ghee
- Raw milk
- Almonds
- Sesame seeds
- Honey

Have warm nut or seed milk, creamy rich soups, and kitcharis. Coconuts, avocados, yams, high quality oils: Coconut, olive, sesame, flax, sunflower, and hemp are the very best. A delicious and ojas-rich meal could be whole grains and lightly cooked vegetables drizzled with oil and sprinkled with freshly toasted nuts and seeds.

Healthy oils will nourish and lubricate your tissues. The fat tissue of your body relates to love. Love yourself physically with warm oil massage and fats in the diet. You will become more juicy. All your foods should be fresh, organic, and prepared lovingly. All foods should be eaten in a sacred way, with conscious awareness.

Ojas-increasing Ayurvedic herbs are the rasayana (rejuvenative) herbs, like:

- Shatavari
- Ashwagandha
- Brahmi
- Licorice
- Guduchi
- Amlaki
- Bala
- Shilajit

Chyavanprash (an herbal jam) is excellent for nourishing ojas. (See resources beginning on page 183.)

Superfoods also nourish ojas. Some examples are:

- Maca
- Spirulina
- Seed and nut milks
- Bee pollen
- Royal jelly
- Elderberry/blueberry/blackberry
- Moringa

Rest, sleep, and deep peaceful meditation increase ojas. The best sleep occurs between 10:00 PM and 4:00 AM. Sleeping after the sun rises or during the day is said to disturb both mind and prana, although a short rest or nap after your mid-day meal is good for digestion, and a short nap in the afternoon could be valuable for a vata type person.

Please review chapter 5 for a reminder of all of the ways that ojas is produced and depleted.

Week Three Overview Rasayana Practices

- Consciously intend to take your life and health to a new level.
- Gently re-introduce a variety of foods that are nourishing and easy to digest.
- Add superfoods to your diet.
- Take tonic & rejuvenative herbs for 2-4 weeks following PK.
- Include lots of healthy oils & fats in your diet.
- Spend time in nature.
- Get plenty of rest.
- Practice conscious breathing.
- Tend to your words and let compassion for yourself and others rise to the top of your consciousness.

- Share loving touch in a healthy way.
- Be gentle with yourself.
- Move your body!

Recommended daily routine for week three ~ rasayana

- Wake with the sun (around 6:00 AM). Give thanks for the day!
- Empty your bladder and bowels.
- Wash your face and rinse your eyes.
- Drink a glass of warm or room temperature water.
- Oil pull.
- Clean your teeth and tongue.
- Gentle yoga, pranayam, meditation.
- Take tonic/rejuvenation herbs before dinner.
- Drink warm spiced nut or seed milk.
- Breakfast.
- Worldly duties (drinking ample water during the day).
- ½ hour before eating lunch have a thin slice of ginger with a little salt to increase agni.
- Lunch (around noon).
- Second work cycle (no drinks for an hour after eating lunch, then resume hot water and/or tea).
- Late afternoon walk.
- Dinner (near 6:00 PM).
- Wind down for bedtime - meditation, calming yoga, calming pranayam, bath, spiritual reading.
- Bedtime before 10:00 PM.

CHAPTER FIFTEEN

~ Be Nourished ~ Recipes for Foods that Heal

Food Guidelines for Cleansing and Rejuvenation

FAVOR	AVOID
Fresh, vital foods	Processed foods
Nutritious, beautiful, & appetizing foods	GMOs, chemicals
An attitude of grateful appreciation	Mindless eating
Easily digested foods (soups, stews)	Fried foods
Steamed or lightly sautéed vegetables	Raw foods in excess
Warm drinks	Cold or carbonated drinks
Whole grains and grain-like seeds (millet, quinoa, buckwheat)	Dairy products
Toasted seeds (sesame, sunflower, pumpkin)	Too many nuts
Small amounts of honey or maple syrup	Refined sugar, aspartame
Digestive spices (ginger, cumin, coriander, fennel)	Meat

There are many different ways to adjust your diet that will initiate a cleansing response. The most typical food used in Ayurveda is kitchari. Being on a mono diet gives the digestive tract a break from having to digest all kinds of foods. However, by continuing to eat, the digestion doesn't shut down like it can when you fast for a period of time.

Each ingredient in kitchari is chosen for its specific quality.

Basic Healing Kitchari Recipe

In a medium (2 quart) stainless steel pot, add:

1 Tbsp. ghee or coconut oil

½ tsp. brown mustard seed

1 tsp. coriander seeds (whole or freshly roasted and ground)

1 tsp. cumin seeds (whole or freshly roasted and ground)

½ tsp. fennel seeds (cooling and balancing for pitta conditions)

Over medium heat, cook seeds until they start to pop.

Add:

2 Tbsp. freshly grated ginger

1 Tbsp. freshly grated turmeric root or 1 tsp. turmeric powder

A pinch of asafetida (aka: hing; it helps reduce gas)

Cook a bit more to meld all the spices together.

Add: 1 cup split mung beans, red lentils, or whole mung beans that have been soaked overnight*

Add: ½ cup of white basmati rice, quinoa, millet, buckwheat, or a mix**

A strip of kombu seaweed (optional)

6 cups of pure water

Bring to a boil, then simmer over medium/low heat for 20 minutes or until completely cooked.

Add vegetables according to cooking time. Use 2-3 cups of mixed veggies: carrots, pumpkin, sweet potatoes, or winter squash, add near the beginning; green beans, summer squash, or broccoli, add maybe 5 minutes before finished; add leafy greens right at the end and immediately turn the heat off.

Salt to taste. Add a spoonful of ghee and a squeeze of lemon or lime to your bowl. Serve with cilantro chutney or freshly chopped cilantro.

* Mung beans, split or whole, are cooling, while red lentils are more warming.

** I like a mixture of basmati rice and quinoa. Or buckwheat and millet. White rice is traditional, as it's easier to digest than brown rice. I like quinoa, millet, and buckwheat because they are more alkaline grains. EXPERIMENT!

Beet & Barley Kitchari

Soak overnight:

1 cup whole mung beans

½ cup pearl barley

Rinse and add to 6 cups pure water.

Add:

1 Tbsp. freshly grated ginger

1 Tbsp. freshly grated turmeric root or 1 tsp. turmeric powder

1 Tbsp. whole cumin seed

2 nice beets cubed (at least 1 cup)

½ - 1 tsp. pure salt

A pinch of black pepper

Follow the same cooking directions for basic kitchari recipe above.

Lemon Dal

1 cup split mung beans or red lentils

½ tsp. brown mustard seed

1 tsp. coriander powder

1 tsp. cumin powder

1 Tbsp. freshly grated ginger root

1 Tbsp. freshly grated turmeric root or 1 tsp. turmeric powder

4 cups pure water

1 tsp. pure salt

Pinch black pepper

Sauté mustard seeds in ghee until they start to pop.

Add other spices and cook together for a minute.

Add rest of ingredients.

Cook for 20 minutes until soft.

Add juice of 1 lemon.

Add ½ cup fresh cilantro just before serving.

Miso Soup

2 cups hot water

1 heaping Tbsp. chickpea miso

1 Tbsp. raw tahini

Stir until miso and tahini are dissolved into the hot water (a whisk works great for this).

Squeeze of lemon or lime.

Miso is a live food. Do not cook it, but add to the water that is already heated and cooled to the point where you can leave your finger in it without burning.

Squish Squash Soup

Put 1 cup barley and a strip of kombu in 5-6 cups of water, cook for half an hour.

Add 2 cups cubed pumpkin or winter squash and continue to cook until very soft.

Squish the squash with a big spoon.

Sauté 1 onion in 2 Tbsp. ghee or coconut oil.

Add:

2 Tbsp. freshly grated ginger root

1 Tbsp. coriander powder (freshly ground is best)

1 Tbsp. whole cumin seeds

2 stalks of celery

1 cup of green beans and a small fresh red pepper

Cook until everything is soft.

Add ½ cup grated coconut.

Garnish with fresh cilantro.

Lemon Rice

Cook 1 cup white or brown basmati rice in 2 cups pure water with a little salt.

When cooked and still hot, add 2 Tbsp. coconut oil or ghee and juice of 1 lemon.

For extra lemon flavor, add some lemon zest.

Drizzled Steamed Veggies

Lightly steam any vegetables you want.

Drizzle with ghee, coconut, or flax oil and a squeeze of lemon or lime.

Sprinkle with gomasio.

Black Bean Soup

Soak 1 ½ cups dry black beans overnight, pour off water in the morning.

Cook beans in 8 cups of water until soft (an hour or so) with:

½ cup brown rice or pearl barley

1 Tbsp. freshly ground cumin seed

1 Tbsp. freshly ground coriander seed

1 tsp. chili powder (or 1 fresh chile and 1-2 cloves of garlic)

A pinch of asafetida

1 Tbsp. salt

Finely chop fresh veggies, focusing on what is in season, and add them according to what takes the longest to cook.

Possibilities:

Carrot

Summer or winter squash

Celery

Tomatoes

Peppers

Onion

Garlic

Fine-tune salt to taste at the end.

Serve with some chopped fresh cilantro.

Beet Coconut Ginger Soup

Steam or boil 2 cups thinly sliced pieces of beet until soft.

Blend with meat from 1 fresh coconut or 1 cup dried shredded coconut.*

Add fresh ginger root - 1" piece.

Add salt to taste.

Garnish with fresh cilantro if you want.

*You could also substitute 1 can of organic coconut milk or some coconut butter.

Coconut Dal

Put 2 tsp. coconut oil in a large sauce pan.

Add ½ - 1 tsp. brown mustard seeds; heat over medium flame until they start popping.

Add:

1 Tbsp. each freshly ground cumin and coriander (whole is fine too)

1 heaping Tbsp. of freshly grated ginger

1 tsp. turmeric powder

2 cups red lentils

6 cups water

1 tsp. salt

Cook until lentils dissolve.

Before serving, add:

1 cup either freshly grated coconut or dried shredded coconut

¼ cup finely chopped cilantro, basil, and/or chives

Adjust salt to taste.

Lemongrass Ginger Coconut Pumpkin Soup

To prepare lemongrass, peel off outside layer of the bulb near the root of the plant, chop very fine, set aside.

Put 2 Tbsp. coconut oil in a pan.

Add ½ tsp each whole coriander seeds and whole mustard seeds; when they start dancing and popping, add and sauté:

2 Tbsp. chopped lemongrass bulb

2 Tbsp. freshly grated ginger root

Add a pinch of asafetida (hing)

Add: 2-3 cups cubed pumpkin or other winter squash and enough pure water to cover

½ - 1 Tbsp. salt (to taste)

Cook until everything is soft and flavors are melded into yummy bliss.

Before serving, add a small handful of chopped, fresh basil and a cup of grated coconut.

Creamy Squash Soup

Cut and cook 3-4 cups pumpkin or winter squash (butternut, delicata, acorn, etc.) in just enough water to cover them, until soft.

Let it cool some and take off skins (you could also peel ahead of time).

In a blender, place:

Cooked and peeled squash

1-2 Tbsp. freshly grated ginger root

¼ tsp. nutmeg

1 cup raw almonds (soaked), cashews, or macadamia nuts

1 tsp. salt

Pinch of pepper

Blend with cooking water to desired consistency.

Ginger-Coconut Yams

Sauté 1 large onion in a little sesame (or other) oil until browned and add 1 ½ inches freshly grated ginger.

Cut up 2-4 cups yams (or winter squash or breadfruit) and add to the sautéed ingredients.

Add 2 cups fresh coconut milk or a can of coconut milk and some salt.

Bake until well cooked, covered, then uncover and caramelize. Yum!

Coconut Milk Subji

Slice vegetables in season, set aside.

Put 1-2 Tbsp. ghee or sesame oil in skillet.

Add 1 tsp. brown mustard seeds, pop.

Add onion, brown.

Add:

2 Tbsp. grated fresh ginger

2 tsp. cumin powder or seeds

2 tsp. coriander powder

1 tsp. turmeric

½ tsp. garam masala (optional)

Add 2 cups fresh coconut milk (coconut meat blended with water and strained) or 1 can coconut milk.

Add veggies, starting with the ones that will require the longest cooking time, continue to add accordingly.

Cover and cook until veggies are completely cooked.

Salt to taste.

North Indian Subji

Sauté 1 chopped onion in ghee or sunflower oil, caramelize.

Add:

- 2 Tbsp. fresh ginger and 2 cloves of garlic, finely chopped
- 1 tsp. garam masala
- 1 tsp. cumin powder
- ½ tsp. turmeric powder
- ½ tsp. salt
- ½ tsp. chili powder (or 1 jalapeño pepper)
- 1 cup water
- 2 tomatoes, chopped
- Veggies of your choice: cauliflower, peas, broccoli, squash, peppers, etc.

Cover and cook until soft. Serve with a light grain.

South Indian Vegetables in Cashew Gravy

Chop an assortment of vegetables to equal 4 cups: carrots, turnips, pumpkin, potato, green beans, peas, etc.

Put 2 Tbsp. ghee or coconut oil in a pan with:

- 1 tsp. brown mustard seeds
- 2 sprigs fresh curry leaves
- 1 tsp. red chile flakes

When it starts to sizzle, add:

- 1 ½ cups cashew milk (raw cashews and water blended until smooth)
- 1 ½ cups chopped tomatoes (or tomato puree)
- Water if needed

Cook until the gravy starts coming away from the sides of the pot.

Add:

2 Tbsp. freshly ground coriander

1 Tbsp. turmeric powder

1 tsp. salt

vegetables

Cover and simmer until vegetables are cooked, stirring occasionally and adding a little water if needed to keep it from sticking to the pot.

Sauté 2 fresh green chiles in 2 Tbsp. ghee (or coconut oil), and fry until golden brown.

Serve on top of vegetables with a bit of freshly chopped cilantro.

Fragrant Spiced South Indian Rice & Quinoa

In 2 Tbsp. ghee or coconut oil, sauté until the fragrances are released:

½ tsp. cardamom seeds (or 8 green pods, cracked)

5 cloves

5 black peppercorns

1 cinnamon stick

1 tsp. fresh finely grated turmeric or turmeric powder

10-12 green curry leaves

Add sautéed spices to:

1 cup basmati rice, rinsed

½ cup quinoa, rinsed

3 cups water

½ tsp. salt

Bring to a boil, then turn down and simmer for 25 minutes.

Kale or Mixed Greens Saag

Steam a big pot of greens (kale or mixed kale, spinach, and mustard greens).

Blend steamed greens with:

1-2 caramelized onions

2 cloves garlic

A chunk of ginger

1 hot chile pepper

Set aside.

Sauté 1 tsp. whole cumin and ½ tsp. fenugreek seeds in coconut oil until toasty.

Add a sprig of fresh curry leaf, cook a bit more.

Combine blended greens and sautéed spices.

Add:

Cumin powder (a good amount for the amount of greens you made!)

A small amount of garam masala

A pinch of asafetida

¼ cup coconut cream

Salt to taste

Zucchini Patties

These delectable delights are a fantastic answer to the late summer zucchini flush. Depending on your meal intention, they can be fashioned after Indian koftas, egg foo young, or even veggie burgers.

Grate 3-4 cups zucchini, drain or squeeze out the excess juice.

Mince ½ or 1 small red onion.

Dice 1 small colorful pepper (sweet or spicy).

Chop ¼ cup fresh cilantro.

1 cup garbanzo flour

1 Tbsp. freshly ground coriander

1 tsp. salt

Mix all ingredients, adding garbanzo flour right before cooking. Form into the shapes you want and brown in a little sunflower or olive oil.

For koftas serve with Fragrant Tomato Curry Sauce. For "egg foo young," add sprouted mung beans and serve with Chinese sweet and sour sauce. For burgers, serve on a bun with your favorite fixin's.

Fragrant Tomato Curry Sauce

In a blender add:

- ½ cup cashews or almonds
- ¼ cup sunflower or sesame seeds
- ½ - 1 inch freshly sliced ginger root
- 1 fresh jalapeño chile, sliced
- 1 Tbsp. freshly ground coriander
- 1 tsp. turmeric powder
- 1 tsp. salt
- ½ tsp. cumin powder
- 2 Tbsp. raw sugar (or 1 Tbsp. agave)
- ¼ cup water or enough to blend all into a thick masala

Chop 2 cups fresh tomatoes (mixed colors are wonderful!).

Toast 1 tsp. brown mustard seed in a little oil (coconut, sunflower, sesame, or olive).

When they are dancing add:

- Tomatoes, masala
- ¼ cup plain yogurt (optional)

Simmer until melded together.

Add ¼ cup chopped fresh cilantro just before serving.

Festive Autumn or Winter Nut Loaf or Patties

Grate 2-3 cups carrots and golden beets (and zucchini if there is still some around).

Drain or squeeze out the excess juice.

Mince ½ or 1 small red onion.

Grind up 1 cup nuts or seeds (walnuts, almonds, hazelnuts, brazil nuts, sunflower, or pumpkin seeds).

Dice 1 small colorful pepper (sweet or spicy).

Chop ¼ cup fresh cilantro.

Add:

1 cup garbanzo flour

1 Tbsp. freshly ground coriander

1 tsp. salt

Mix all ingredients, adding garbanzo flour right before cooking. Either press into a loaf pan and bake at 350° for an hour or so, or shape into patties and brown in a little olive, sunflower, or sesame oil.

Spicy Burdock Root

Wash and peel burdock root, cut into julienne slices. (To maintain color, put in water with apple cider vinegar or lemon juice.)

Lightly toast brown mustard, coriander, fennel, and fenugreek seeds - grind.

Pour 2-4 Tbsp. ghee or coconut oil into a pan (depending on how much burdock root you have).

Add ground spices plus a pinch of asafetida.

Add a little finely grated ginger and turmeric,

Sauté burdock until tender (adding a little water if needed).

At the end, add a splash of tamari and brown a little.

Coconut Green Beans

Melt 1 Tbsp. coconut oil in a frying pan.

Pop 1 tsp. mustard seeds in the oil.

Add a pinch of asafetida and a pinch of salt.

Lightly sauté green beans in the spice masala.

For an extra rich treat, add a spoonful of coconut cream just before serving.

Green Bean Nut Sunnie Pâté

2 cups green beans, cooked

½ cup nuts (walnuts, cashews, brazil nuts, or almonds)

½ cup sunflower seeds

Cold-pressed oil (olive, sesame, sunflower)

½ tsp. salt

Pinch black pepper

¼ tsp. nutmeg

Grind all in a food processor.

Muesli

2 ½ cups rolled oats

¼ cup sunflower seeds

⅛ cup (or 2 Tbsp.) each flax seeds and chia seeds

⅛ cup (or 2 Tbsp.) dried cherries (raisins, chopped dried pears, or apricots)

6 dates cut into small pieces

A pinch of cardamom, cinnamon, nutmeg, or any or all of the above

Mix together all ingredients. To serve, add either warm water or any kind of milk, let soak for a few minutes, and enjoy with or without a little sweetener.

Hot Cereal

Rice cream, oatmeal, quinoa, millet, or buckwheat all make delicious breakfast foods.

Cook grains until soft in three times as much water as grain.

When cooked, add:

- Ghee
- Milk of choice
- Ground cardamom
- Cinnamon
- Nutmeg
- Ginger

Sweetener of choice: honey, maple syrup, or dates

Or for savory cereal use masala (spice) mix (churna)

Or raw tahini and chickpea miso

Sour Cereal

12 cups pure water

2 cups quinoa or rice

1 cup red lentils

Bring to a boil, then cook over medium heat until soft.

Blend together:

- 1-2 tomatoes
- 6 dates
- 1 cup coconut
- 2 jalapeño peppers
- 1 bunch green onions (optional)
- 1 Tbsp. cumin (whole or powder)
- 1 Tbsp. fenugreek

Blend, add to pot, cook some more.

Add salt to taste.

Beet Apple Salad or Chutney

This delicious combination has specific healing qualities and intentions:

Beets for thinning the bile.

Apples for helping soften or dissolve stones that may be forming in the liver or gall bladder.

Cilantro for heavy metal detoxification.

Fresh ginger for increasing the digestive fire.

Lime or lemon for alkalizing the system.

Grate roughly equal amounts of beet and apple.

Add:

Ample chopped cilantro (About ½ cup per 1 cup beet/apple mix)

1 tsp. finely grated fresh ginger

Juice of ½ fresh lime or lemon

Creamy Dreamy Beet Raita

Beets

Plain yogurt

Dill weed or seed

Dice fresh beets in whatever size appeals to you. Boil or steam them until tender. Allow to cool. Toss with plain yogurt and add a small amount of dill weed or seed to taste.

This is a delightfully sweet and sour salad.

Coconut-Cashew Hummus

Soak 1 cup dry garbanzo beans in a quart of water overnight, drain.

Cook either in a pressure cooker or on the stove top until thoroughly cooked in 6 cups water.

In 2 Tbsp. coconut oil, sauté 2 tsp. cumin seeds and a pinch of asafetida.

Add: ¾ cup raw cashews and sauté for a couple of minutes.

Near the end, add 2 Tbsp. freshly grated ginger root and 1 Tbsp. freshly grated turmeric or 1 tsp. turmeric powder.

Pureé garbanzo beans and spiced cashews with:

¾ cup coconut milk
3 Tbsp. lime juice
Salt to taste (start with ½ tsp.)
A little black pepper

Stir in ½ cup chopped cilantro.

Vegan Deluxe Waldorf Salad

Celery, sliced
Apple, chopped
Pecans (and/or walnuts, almonds, etc.)
Dates (and/or raisins, dried cherries, currants)
Sprinkle with lime or lemon juice.
Dress with cashew cream.

Cashew Cream

1 cup cashews (almonds or macadamia nuts)
2 Tbsp. coconut oil
A quick squirt of agave nectar or a tsp. of honey
A little water

Blend until creamy dreamy delicious.

Superfood Fruit Salad

Start by harvesting or gathering together small amounts of fresh herbs. I like:

Basil

Mint

Parsley

Cilantro

Gather edible flowers. In my garden I always grow:

Calendula (petals are edible)

Impatiens

Nasturtiums

Borage

Chop up your favorite fruit (or what you have on hand!).

Pineapple

Grapefruit

Papaya

Apples

Tangerines

Bananas

Fresh berries (strawberry, blueberry, blackberry)

Toss with the herbs, garnish with the flowers.

Sprinkle with some chopped nuts or sunflower seeds, chopped dates or raisins.

Blend together some coconut butter and lime juice with a little hot water.

Add a little sweetener if you want.

Freshly grind some flax and/or chia seeds.

Sprinkle with some cacao nibs.

WOW!

This salad is full of minerals!

Take it in … fully.

Nut or Seed "Milk"

Nut or Seed "Milk" is an alternative to milk, but just as rich and ojas-building.

Soak 1 cup of nuts or seeds (almonds, macadamia nuts, cashews, Brazil nuts, pecans, sunflower seeds, sesame seeds) overnight with about 1 quart water.

Blend on high speed until liquefied. Add more water if it's too thick (depending on what kind of nut or seed you used).

Strain through a fine strainer into another container, or if you want it thicker, skip this step, then pour back into blender. Add a little honey, maple syrup, or stevia and a little almond or vanilla extract (if you like).

Mango Lassi

Blend nut milk or plain yogurt and water with organic mango and a pinch of cardamom (and turmeric). YUM!

Dr. Lad's Hot Almond Milk Recipe for Building Ojas

Soak 10 almonds in a cup of water overnight.

Peel and put in a blender with:

1 cup warm milk (nondairy milk is ok too)

1 tsp. date or coconut sugar, honey, or maple syrup (or a couple of dates!)

A pinch of cardamom

A pinch of ginger powder

1 tsp. ghee

Blend and enjoy!

Here's to strong ojas!

Golden Milk

Blend:

¼ cup almonds, cashews, or sesame seeds (preferably soaked)

2 dates

1 tsp. ghee

A slice or 2 of fresh ginger and turmeric root

A pinch of cardamom

Cactus Cooler

In the blender:

2-4 inches of a fresh aloe leaf, peeled

Insides of 2-3 passion fruit or 1 cup berries

1 quart hibiscus tea that has cooled

Honey or agave to taste

Blend and Relax ... Enjoy!

Superfood Smoothie

¼ cup almonds, cashews, or macadamia nuts

1 Tbsp. maca

1 tsp. shatavari or ashwagandha powder

½ tsp. spirulina powder

1 banana and/or ½ cup fresh berries (blueberries, blackberries, strawberries, raspberries, or mixed!)

1-2 dates

1 Tbsp. coconut or flax oil

2 cups pure water

Blend until smooth.

Serve at room temperature!

Caffeine-Free Masala Chai

1 cup freshly grated ginger

3 cinnamon sticks

20 green cardamom pods

6 clove buds

6 black peppercorns

1 gallon water

Bring to a boil, then simmer down 15 minutes or more to desired strength.

Add your choice of milk and sweetener.

Ram Priya Dass's Himalayan Chai

Grate a large handful (maybe 1 cup) of fresh ginger and add to 8 cups pure water.

Bring to a boil, then simmer for 15 minutes or so.

Grind a small palmful (1-2 Tbsp.) of whole cardamom pods with a mortar and pestle or in a spice grinder. Add to ginger and turn heat off.

Dry roast some loose Darjeeling tea over a low flame just until fragrant and starting to smoke. (Do not burn!)

Add to masala (spice mix) and steep for 2 minutes ONLY.

Strain immediately into another pot.

Add an equal amount of milk and add sugar to taste. Bring to a simmering boil and ENJOY!

There are many delightful variations, like cinnamon in the cold season or mint, tulsi, or cacao. Yummy!

Ojas Balls

In a small food processor, add:

1 cup raw cashews

2 Tbsp. ghee

2-3 pitted dates

½ tsp. ground cardamom

Grind and form into balls, refrigerate, covered.

Superfood Bliss Balls

Mix, match, and experiment.

Nut butters: tahini, almond, cashew, sunflower

Sweeteners: dates, honey, agave, maple syrup

Choose from any of these superfoods:

Spirulina

Shatavari or ashwagandha powder

Royal jelly powder (freeze-dried)

Bee pollen

Maca

Organic cacao powder

Goji berries, raisins, dried ginger pieces

Hemp seeds

Mix well, roll into balls (with prayer, intention, and mantra!).

Coat with coconut, cacao powder, or sesame seeds.

Coconut Barley Pudding

Soak 1 cup pearl barley overnight. Drain and put in a pot with 2 ½ cups water; bring to a boil, and simmer on low for 40 minutes.

When it is cooked well, add:

2 cans organic full fat coconut milk

½ cup organic raw sugar (light, not dark)

1 tsp. vanilla, ground or extract

A touch of cinnamon, nutmeg, or cardamom as you wish

Organic raisins, dried cherries, or dates

Cook, stirring occasionally over medium heat until nice and thick.

Allow to cool.

Serve with toasted coconut over the top.

Maha Squash Anand

~ Great Squash Bliss~

Whip ¼ cup butter and ¼ cup coconut oil together with ½ cup raw sugar and a little vanilla.

Add 2 cups steamed mashed winter squash or pumpkin.

Mix together.

Add:

1 cup spelt flour

½ tsp. of salt

1 tsp. (Non-aluminum) baking powder

Mix together and put into a buttered baking dish.

Make a crumbly topping with nuts, butter, spices (cardamom, cinnamon), and sugar, and sprinkle it on top.

Bake at 350 until browned.

Oh my!

Cilantro Coconut Chutney

Wash and chop 2 cups fresh cilantro.

Add:

2 Tbsp. fresh ginger root

1 cup fresh or dried grated coconut

A dollop of Maple Syrup

Lime or lemon Juice

A little salt

Buzz up in small food processor or blender.

Tamarind Rose Mint Chutney

Add water to dried tamarind to make it the consistency of pea soup, remove all the seeds; chop fresh mint and some fresh pink rose petals, add honey, maple syrup, or sugar to taste.

Coconut Tomato Chutney

Put 2 Tbsp. coconut oil in a frying pan over a medium heat.

Add:

½ tsp. brown mustard seeds

½ tsp. cumin seeds

When they start to dance and pop, add:

5-6 green curry leaves

1-2 fresh or dry red chiles (adjust to heat tolerance level)

½ tsp. turmeric

Pinch of asafetida

1 ½ Tbsp. finely chopped ginger

2 medium tomatoes (about 1 cup chopped tomatoes)

1 tsp. salt (adjust to taste)

2 Tbsp. chopped cilantro

3 Tbsp. freshly grated coconut or dried shredded coconut

Cook until it becomes one delicious thing.

Peach, Pineapple, or Mango Chutney

In 2 Tbsp. sesame or coconut oil, gently sauté:

½ tsp. mustard seeds

½ tsp. cumin seeds

Add:

1 Tbsp. freshly grated ginger (or 1 tsp. powdered)

½ tsp. turmeric powder

Cook a few minutes to meld flavors.

Add 2 cups sliced or diced fruit: peaches, pineapple, or mangoes, and continue cooking until a little browned.

Add:

1 Tbsp. water

¼ tsp. salt

1 tsp. honey if needed

1 red chile if you want it hot.

Sweet Mung Beans

Soak 1 cup whole mung beans overnight.

Cook mung beans in water with a little salt until done.

When fully cooked, add:

1 can of coconut milk (or its equivalent, fresh even better!)

1 Tbsp. finely grated ginger

Ground sweet spices of your choosing: cinnamon, cardamom, nutmeg

½ tsp. turmeric powder

2 Tbsp. sweetener of your choosing: maple syrup, sucanat, honey

Gomasio

Dry roast 1 cup whole brown sesame seeds (in their hull) until fragrant.

Grind in a large mortar and pestle or spice grinder.

Add ½ tsp. salt and mix well.

Vata Balancing Churna

Grind into a fine powder, mix together, and store in a tightly sealed jar.

3 Tbsp. coriander seed
2 Tbsp. fennel seed
2 Tbsp. turmeric powder
2 Tbsp. cardamom seed
1 Tbsp. cumin seed
1 Tbsp. brown mustard seed
1 Tbsp. ginger powder
1 Tbsp. cinnamon powder

Pitta Balancing Churna

Grind into a fine powder, mix together, and store in a tightly sealed jar.

2 Tbsp. fennel seed
3 Tbsp. coriander seed
2 Tbsp. turmeric powder
2 Tbsp. cardamom seed
1 Tbsp. cumin seed

Kapha Balancing Churna

Grind into a fine powder, mix together, and store in a tightly sealed jar.

2 Tbsp. cumin seed

1 Tbsp. coriander seed

1 Tbsp. fennel seed

1 Tbsp. brown mustard seed

1 Tbsp. fenugreek seed

2 Tbsp. turmeric powder

1 Tbsp. ginger powder

1 Tbsp. cinnamon powder

1 Tbsp. cardamom seed powder

½ tsp. cloves

½ tsp. cayenne powder

Garam Masala

Grind and store in a tightly sealed jar.

2 Tbsp. cinnamon

2 Tbsp. cardamom

2 Tbsp. clove buds

2 Tbsp. black peppercorns

Ghee

Another supreme and revered food in Ayurveda is ghee. Ghee is taken internally to lubricate the tissues from the inside.

Ghee is no longer considered a dairy product, as it has had all the lactose and casein removed, leaving behind only a clear, high quality medicinal oil that is a rich source of omega 3 and 9 EFA's and anti-oxidants. Ghee is balancing for dryness because it is unctuous (oily); balancing for heat and inflammation because it is cooling; and it carries the properties of any herbs or spices used with it into the deeper tissues of the body.

Ghee Meditation
(as taught by Bri. Maya Tiwari)

To prepare 1 pint of ghee:

Open your senses and be fully present while preparing your ghee.

Take 1 pound of organic unsalted (cultured) butter and melt it over medium heat.

Do not stir the ghee at any time during this process. The ghee will bubble and foam at first, making a lot of sound like rain on a tin roof. You will notice the sounds changing as the ghee goes through its transformation. The rain will become lighter; then it will sound like a singing stream, then a babbling brook. Then the ghee will get really quiet. You know it's almost done ... the solids will have fallen to the bottom of the pan, forming a crust that is golden brown. Turn it off and let it cool some. Your ghee is now ready to strain.

Remove any foam that remains on the top with a slotted spoon and pour the ghee through a couple of thicknesses of fine cheesecloth or a fine sieve. You will have a pure golden liquid in the end. Store in a jar or crock in the fridge or at room temperature. Be careful not to dip into your ghee with a wet or dirty spoon. Water or traces of food will contaminate your ghee.

Herbalized Ghee

Often a quite bitter medicinal ghee called Tikta Ghrita is taken for internal oleation. You can buy this from a few different sources online. I would suggest consulting with an Ayurvedic practitioner to receive some guidance on amounts to take, based on an evaluation of your agni, however. This is a very potent medicated ghee.

Or, you may want to experiment with some simpler herbal infused ghee recipes.

Making this may be too much for most people, but if you're

feeling adventurous, you may decoct spices that aid digestion into your ghee to make a wonderful healing substance.

Make a strong herbal decoction by adding herbs to water, bringing to a boil, and then turning down to a simmer until a lot of the water has cooked away. Strain and add to ghee. Bring this mixture up to a simmer and cook until all of the water has evaporated. You will be able to tell because when there is water in the ghee, it will bubble profusely. When the water has cooked out, it will still be bubbling, but you will notice a distinct change in the quality of the bubbles if you are paying attention.

When making an herbal ghee for taking internally during a cleanse, I use the main spices used to balance digestion: cumin, coriander, fennel, ginger, turmeric.

To make the ghee more heating to enkindle the digestive fire, you could leave out the fennel and add more ginger, turmeric, cinnamon, cardamom, and black pepper.

To make it more cooling and cleansing for the liver, you can add burdock, dandelion root, milk thistle, or neem.

A ghee for calming the mind and nervous system could have brahmi or gotu kola added.

A women's adaptogenic tonic ghee can be made with shatavari, which is a cooling tonic and a hormone precursor.

A men's adaptogenic tonic ghee can be made with ashwagandha, a warming tonic herb. Both of these adaptogenic tonic ghees can be used for either men or women; they just have specific effects for men or women as well as many other beneficial qualities.

Adaptogens help you deal with stress more easily. There are many adaptogenic herbs. It warrants some research, as these can really help you at this time when there are many stressors coming from the environment and also stress from simply living in the world at this time. We are designed to live in nature. To the degree that we are disconnected from that, we are stressed.

CHAPTER SIXTEEN

Sadhana ~ Daily Practices for Elevating Radiance

We have arrived at the closing chapter of this book and the opening to a whole new chapter in life! I pray that this offering will touch and enhance your life in many beneficial ways.

What will serve you in the deepest way is engaging in self-care practices on a regular basis: daily, weekly, monthly. These practices nurture your body, mind, and heart and reveal your true self, the essential nature of your soul.

There are many Ayurvedic books that outline an ideal daily routine or "dinacharya." The stumbling block I have encountered when I see some of these is that I know it doesn't fit into MY day. So I have, in the past, let go of even trying. In realizing that my daily routine is the ground beneath me, I have designed a routine that works for me, now.

It's been helpful for me to take a small step towards developing new habits and master that step, then re-evaluate and integrate another. If you have been unsuccessful before, try this and see if you can make small changes that add up to truly significant lifestyle changes. In a few short months, you can look back and see how much you have shifted and how much better you feel! It's so rewarding.

Also, if (or WHEN!) you slip, just turn and resume. It's really that simple. No guilt, no shame, just take another step in the direction that supports you.

Recommended Ayurvedic daily routine

- Wake with the sun (around 6:00 AM)
- Give thanks for the day!
- Wash your face and rinse your eyes
- Drink a glass of warm or room temperature water
- Empty your bowels
- Scrape your tongue
- Oil pull
- Clean your teeth and tongue
- Nasya
- Oil massage
- Bath or shower
- Exercise
- Pranayam
- Meditation
- Breakfast (by 8:00 AM)
- Worldly duties (work)
- Lunch (around noon)
- After lunch or after work take a walk
- Dinner (near 6:00 PM)
- Wind down for bedtime - light media, calming yoga, pranayam, bath, spiritual reading, and/or meditation
- Bedtime before 10:00 PM

As you look at this ideal daily routine, no doubt you will compare it to what you are currently doing. Please be gentle with yourself! Look for ways that you can adjust your habits to integrate one or two of these practices. Once integrated, add another until your daily habits are transformed into a beautiful self-nurturing daily routine.

The timing of these activities is in concert with the circadian rhythms of the earth. By aspiring to live generally within these time considerations, you are aligning yourself with nature and will therefore be naturally more supported in your life. For instance, as I said in a previous chapter, the digestive fire is strongest around the noon hour when the sun is highest. And, if you finish eating 3 hours before bedtime, your liver will be able to filter and process more efficiently while you sleep. Your sleep will be more sound, and you will actually be able to arise a little earlier!

Weekly Fast

A fast on high quality liquids once a week is a wonderful practice to reset your appetites. Please take this day of fasting to get a bit more rest and engage in gentle activities.

- In the morning start with a warm drink, either warm water with lemon, tea, or warm nut milk.
- During the day and into the evening, have plenty of water.
- When you need some nourishment, have:

  Golden Milk (Almond, cashew, or sesame milk with a date or 2, a spoonful of ghee, a little ginger and turmeric, and a pinch of cardamom)

  A Superfood Smoothie (room temperature!)

  Fresh juice

  Miso soup

Monthly Basti

The basti (herbal enema) is a wonderful way to nourish and/or cleanse yourself once a month.

- To reduce vata and add strength and stability, you could simply use ½ cup sesame oil or you could make a tonic tea with ashwagandha and milk (with added sesame oil).
- To cleanse and clear, use dashmool decoction and/or triphala tea.
- To activate and detoxify your liver's function, use coffee, green or roasted blond.

Working with Your Subtle Energies

Prana, tejas, and ojas are the Sanskrit words for the reflection of the Absolute Being as: Life-Light-Love or Being-Consciousness-Bliss, or Sat (truth)-Chit (pure consciousness)-Ananda (perfect bliss).

Prana is the vital life force energy. Because we live in the three dimensional world which is subject to the law of gravity, prana tends to gravitate to the lower chakras (energy centers) of the body early on one's evolutionary path. Ideally, you want to live with all of your chakras activated and switched on.

The root chakra relates to our "tribe" or family of origin, survival, and the "race-mind" or cultural consciousness. If your energy is blocked or concentrated in this center, you may find your energy tied up with the daily grind of survival and/or be overly concerned about conforming to your cultural/familial "norms."

The second chakra is often referred to as the sexual center. If your energy is concentrated here, you will be overly engaged in the pursuit of sex or money. If it is blocked here, you may be shut down, unsuccessful, or disinterested in these aspects of life.

The third chakra is the center of one's power. If your energy is concentrated here, you will be focused on the pursuit of power. If this center is blocked, you may feel fearful or gullible, with a lack of will or healthy boundaries.

The fourth center is the heart chakra. When you activate your heart center and live "from" here, you naturally expand compassion and empathy. You become capable of Love, unconditional love in all of its attributes: affection, devotion, patience, kindness, and generosity. When your heart center is open, the pranic (life force) energy can easily rise, and the higher centers also activate.

The fifth center is the throat chakra. Your throat center can become a magnificent tool for communicating your heart with the spoken word or song.

The sixth center is the third eye chakra. The third eye becomes activated, and your intuition becomes more available as a guiding force in your life. And magically, the thoughts that are generated from your crown chakra become more refined, more life-affirming, and more creative. YES! The quality of your thoughts CAN change!

The seventh center is the crown chakra. The crown chakra is a generator of thoughts. Many many many more thoughts than you can even pick up on. Most of these go into the subconscious mind where they subtly coagulate into your self-image. It is this self-image that is magnetizing life experiences to you; like the people you meet, the opportunities that come your way, even the ideas you have, and certainly the beliefs you hold about what is possible for you.

As you engage in the practices outlined in this book, you may actually be releasing some of the subconscious material that has been running you. This is powerful! You have the capacity to transform the vibrational quality of the thoughts that occur to you! Then, your whole life will change. Consider this as an invitation to play with your consciousness and prove your own power to yourself.

By activating your higher energy centers and becoming more and more at home on the throne of your inner being, you can engage each of your senses in healing and balancing yourself and perhaps inspire those within your sphere of influence.

Here are some ways that you can play with your senses to elevate your vibrational frequency. Practice often!

Sound

Sound relates to ether. You sense sound with your ears, and you generate sound with your mouth.

Breathe! Simply consciously breathing while intentionally focusing on your heart or third eye is remarkably effective for allowing the rise of pranic energy. Energy follows intention and attention.

Observe times of silence.

Listen to your own heart.

Practice meditation.

Become aware of your inner story.

Chanting, repeating mantra, or singing replaces mind chatter.

Listen to healing music.

Listen to the sounds of nature with full attention.

Touch

Touch relates to air. You sense touch with your skin and give touch with your hands.

Activate heightened presence in your hands.

When you touch someone, including yourself, pay extra attention and perhaps offer a silent intention. When you touch someone or something, you have the opportunity to make it a transmission of love. Healing chemicals are enlivened in the physiology when we touch or are touched lovingly. Massage has so many benefits: increased flow of life force energy, blood circulation, increased lymph flow. Plus, it's nourishing for the skin and feeds the soul.

Massage oils for grounding, calming, and balancing vata are warm and heavier, like sesame & almond oils. Adding warm, sweet, heavier essential oils will further promote balance.

Massage oils for cooling and calming pitta are a little lighter and cooling in nature: coconut, olive, ghee, and sunflower fit in this category. The addition of sweet, cooling, and heavier floral essential oils will further balance pitta.

Massage oils for stimulating and balancing kapha are warming, light oils like mustard oil and safflower oil. The addition of pungent, stimulating aromas will enhance the desired effect.

Sight

Sight relates to the element fire/light. We sense light with the eyes, and Ayurveda says the organ of action is the feet because they can take us to different sights.

Beauty and order are healing, sattvic, calming, and seen everywhere in the natural world

Create or gaze upon beautiful mandalas. Mandalas are most often circular designs with a repeating pattern. They are everywhere in nature. Awaken to the mandalas that are all around you, often unnoticed. Look at the seed patterns when you slice open a fruit or vegetable, for instance. Gaze upon the patterns in a leaf or flower. Patterns of beauty are literally all around and within us!

Colors – Start noticing how different colors evoke different feeling states in you.

The Ayurvedic teaching about colors is that vata balancing colors are warm and calming "sattvic" colors like rose, lavender, gold, and magenta.

Pitta balancing colors are cool and calming "sattvic" colors like turquoise, aqua, sky blue, and shades of green.

Kapha balancing colors are bright and stimulating colors like orange, red, yellow, and hot pink.

How do different colors affect how you feel?

Open yourself to receiving the prana that is available in the natural world, a true feast for the eyes. There is such an abundance of constant beauty in the trees, flowers, birdsongs, the movement of water, wind, the play of sunlight on the water. It's endless and infinite, really.

Meditate on a sacred symbol, a flower, or a candle.

You can also care for your eyes by doing regular eye washes. You can make a gentle tea to wash your eyes with organic rose petals, chrysanthemum flowers, or triphala powder (be sure to strain thoroughly).

Have a Netra Basti occasionally with a practitioner or friend-(Ayurvedic eye bath with ghee).

Taste

Taste relates to the element of water. The sense organ is the tongue. The organ of action is said to be the urethra as in "making water."

When you drink, become fully present to receive what you're taking into your body.

Honor your water as sacred. Increase the energetic healing properties of water with gratitude and intention. Drink ample water, as pure as you can find. Avoid carbonated water.

Cleanse your tongue daily. When you use a tongue scraper, or even a spoon to cleanse ama from your tongue first thing in the morning, you are simultaneously massaging the organs associated with each area of your tongue. There is a lot of information that an Ayurvedic practitioner can tell you from looking at your tongue.

Cracking, discoloration, or sensitivity of a particular area of the tongue indicates a disorder in the organ corresponding to that area. The size, shape, and color as well as the color of the coating on your tongue all provide clues to what is happening on the inside.

Smell

Smell relates to the element earth. The sense organ is, of course, your nose. According to Ayurveda, the organ of action is the anus (the releasing of gaseous smells.)

Ayurveda says that the nose is the doorway to the brain.

Scents can evoke memories and leave lasting impressions.

Each of us has unique interpretations of any given aroma based on our life experiences with them.

The scent of lavender may bring one person to a sense of warmth and comfort because it reminds them of their beloved grandmother. For another, it may conjure up an unpleasant memory. It's delightful to have at least a small array of high quality, pure essential oils in your home to be able to add to a bath or a spritzer bottle filled with pure water.

Your nose is a great organ that protects you from potentially harmful substances. Listen to your own discernment about what smells evoke a sense of calm well-being. Which essential oils are the most valuable for you? Ayurveda has some general guidelines about aromatics, but the bottom line is how YOU feel about them. When using essential oils on your skin, it's good to first put down a carrier oil, as some essential oils are so powerful that they may burn. Do your research!

To balance vata: Warm, sweet, heavy scents like:
vanilla, amber, sweet orange, rose, lavender, sandalwood

To balance pitta: Cool, heavy scents like:
gardenia, jasmine, frangipani, rose, lavender, sandalwood

To balance kapha: Warm, stimulating, light scents like:
eucalyptus, cedar, sage, tulsi, patchouli, lavender, sandalwood

Some Last Thoughts on Lifestyle...

Make time for play! It is beneficial for you, no matter who you are, to get your energy activated every day. MOVE and BREATHE! Sing, garden, walk, swim, bike ride, do some asana practice, take up a Qi gong practice, a Tai Chi practice, dance, whatever makes you come alive!

Cherish your relationships. Give them ample attention and praise. Life is a mirror, and what you put out is reflected back to you. As you uplift others, you will also get carried on that buoyancy.

Your body and nervous system thrive with routine. Open your awareness to the rhythms of nature, the seasons and times of day, and establish your own rhythms that are in harmony with the cosmos. You are a child of the universe; your body is a gift that allows you to experience, express, create, learn, and expand in all the ways you can imagine.

Please use this information to uplift your life. There is so much here. Return to it occasionally, and notice how you are evolving your understanding of life and yourself.

If you are new to Ayurveda, know that my greatest hope is that this offering will inspire you to continue to study and practice. Please, do not attempt to offer panchakarma to others unless and until you have had a complete education in Ayurveda.

If you are a practitioner or teacher of Ayurveda, may this book serve as a teaching tool for your students and may it enkindle a passion for this practice.

Truly, this life is nothing less than a miracle!

CHAPTER SEVENTEEN

Cleanse at a Glance

Week One Overview

- Clear your time and create sacred space for yourself.
- Identify and write out an intention for your cleanse.
- Be in silence, reflecting inwardly as much as you can.
- Eat kitchari as much as you're able to or a clean, whole food, fat-free diet (recipe on page 136).
- Eat Beet Apple Cilantro Salad frequently (recipe on page 151).
- Drink blood cleansing teas, 2-3 cups each day. (page 104)
- Sip hot water throughout the day every 10-15 mins.
- Drink lemon water, minimum 1 quart daily.
- Do oil pulling daily (page 105).
- Internal oleation daily for 5 days (page 105).
- Massage warmed oil into your skin daily, followed by a hot bath or shower and wrap (pages 106-107).

Week Two Overview

- Do abhyanga (page 55)/swedana (page 56) daily until you complete the virechana and bastis.
- Do virechana (purge) on a day that you can REST THE FOLLOWING DAY (page 112)!
- Samsarjana krama (rebuilding digestive fire) followed by a day of rest (page 114).
- Next, begin bastis, starting and ending with oil basti, doing herbal or coffee basti daily between (pages 115-119).
- Ama-reducing diet (page 71) and blood cleansing teas (page 104).
- Neti (page 76) and/or nasya (page 54), oiling the nostrils daily.
- Do cleansing pranayam daily: bhastrika, kapalabhati, or the simple yogic cleansing breath (pages 98-99).
- Shanka prakshalana asanas daily or some asanas that twist and press your belly (pages 119-124).
- Be in silence as much as you can.
- Rest and reflect on your intention as much as you can.

Week Three Overview
Rasayana Practices

- Consciously intend to take your life and health to a new level.
- Gently re-introduce a variety of foods that are nourishing and easy to digest.
- Add superfoods to your diet.
- Take tonic & rejuvenative herbs for 2-4 weeks following PK.
- Include lots of healthy oils & fats in your diet.
- Spend time in nature.
- Get plenty of rest.
- Practice conscious breathing.
- Tend to your words and let compassion for yourself and others rise to the top of your consciousness.
- Share loving touch in a healthy way.
- Be gentle with yourself.
- Move your body!

So many Blessings to you as you explore
this path of Supreme Self Care!

With All My Love,
Myrica Morningstar

Ayurvedic Shopping List

Please invest in your excellent health and procure organic, non-GMO foods and spices.

Bulk foods:

Almonds (raw)
Basmati rice, brown and white
Black beans (dry)
Buckwheat (raw)
Cashews (raw)
Garbanzo beans
Millet
Mung beans, whole and split
Oats (rolled, not quick)
Pine nuts (raw)
Quinoa
Red lentils
Sesame seeds (brown and black)
Sunflower seeds (raw)
Walnuts

Oils:

Ghee (Ancient Organics)
Coconut oil (cold-pressed extra virgin)
Sunflower oil
Sesame oil, raw and toasted
(toasted is great in stir fry for a change... just a little!)
Olive oil

Spices:

- Asafetida
- Brown mustard seeds (whole)
- Black peppercorns
- Cardamom
- Cayenne powder
- Cinnamon
- Cloves
- Coriander (whole seeds)
- Cumin (whole seeds)
- Curry leaves
- Curry powder
- Fennel seed
- Fenugreek seed
- Ginger (fresh and powder)
- Marjoram
- Nutmeg
- Oregano
- Rosemary
- Saffron
- Thyme
- Turmeric (fresh root and powder)

Veggies in Season:

- Basil
- Beans (green)
- Beets (red & golden)
- Bok choy
- Broccoli
- Brussels sprouts
- Burdock root (gobo)
- Cabbage (green & purple)
- Carrots
- Cauliflower
- Cilantro

- Chard (rainbow)
- Eggplant
- Fennel
- Kale
- Onions (green, yellow, red)
- Peas
- Peppers (sweet and spicy)
- Potatoes (yellow and red)
- Pumpkin
- Summer squash
- Winter squash (butternut, acorn, delicata)
- Yams

Fruits in Season

- Apples
- Bananas
- Berries (strawberries, blueberries, blackberries)
- Coconut
- Lemons
- Limes
- Mangos
- Oranges
- Papaya
- Passion fruit
- Pineapple
- Starfruit
- Tamarind

Dried Fruits

- Apricots
- Berries
- Cherries
- Currants
- Dates
- Figs
- Raisins

Miscellaneous

Balsamic vinegar
(I love the Grand Reserve by Napa Valley Naturals)
Braggs Liquid Aminos
Coconut aminos
Coconut
Coconut milk (Native Forest)
Garbanzo bean flour
Honey (raw, local to you)
Maple syrup
Miso (Miso Master organic chickpea is my favorite)
Olives (a variety)
Pasta (brown rice is my fav and gluten free)
Salt (pink Himalayan, earth salt, or sea salt from a clean source)
Seaweeds (from Maine)
Spelt flour
Tamari

Superfoods

Bee pollen
BioLumina Spirulina (see resources starting on page 183)
Cacao powder and nibs
Hemp hearts
Maca powder
Royal jelly

Resources

Me!
Myrica Morningstar
PO Box 1019
Kilauea, Hawaii 96754
808-346-1074
myrica@ayurvedabliss.org
www.ayurvedabliss.org

- **Kitchari Kits** (just add water and veggies!)

  All Organic Traditional Kitchari - split mung beans, white basmati rice, ginger, turmeric, cumin, coriander, mustard seed, Himalayan salt, black pepper

  All Organic Light & Savory Kitchari - split mung beans, millet, white basmati rice, ginger, turmeric, cumin, cardamom, green curry leaf, pink Himalayan salt, black pepper

  All Organic Grain Free Superfood Kitchari - red lentils, millet, buckwheat, ginger, turmeric, burdock root, cumin, coriander, mustard seed, fennel seed, moringa leaf, holy basil, chaga powder, Himalayan salt, black pepper

- **Super Sattvic Nasya Drops** (rose, sandalwood, holy basil, eucalyptus, and cardamom in coconut and sunflower oil)

- **Sun Worshippers Skin Elixir** - A luscious cream rejuvenator for your skin.

  Contains:

  Shatavari, bringraj, turmeric, neem, amlaki, brahmi, calendula infused in sunflower/sesame oil, almond oil, vitamin E oil , coconut oil, shea butter, aloe vera gel, rose water, beeswax

- **Silky Skin Body Powder** - A lovely body wash, used alone or after abhyanga to remove oil. Also used for udvartana powder (add a little salt and mix with oil until nut butter consistency).

  Contains:

  Chickpea flour, barley flour, rose powder, red sandalwood powder, frankincense powder, nutmeg

  General use for face or body:

  For vata, mix with oil
  For pitta, mix with milk
  For kapha, mix with warm water

  Apply in small upward circular motions to your face.

  For the whole body, add salt and use as a vigorous scrub stroking towards your heart.

- **BioLumina Spirulina** - (The best on the planet) www.newphoenixrising.com/morningstar

- **Banyan Botanicals -**
  Bulk herbs, Ayurvedic herbal tablets, herbal oils, and great information!
  www.banyanbotanicals.com

- **Tri Health Ayurveda -**
  Authentic herbal oils from Kerala, India
  www.oilbath.com

Education

The Ayurvedic Institute
Albuquerque, New Mexico
www.ayurveda.com/education

The California College of Ayurveda
Nevada City, California
www.ayurvedacollege.com

Northwest Institute of Ayurveda
Arcata, California
www.ayurvedicliving.com

Mount Madonna Institute
Watsonville, California
www.mountmadonnainstitute.org

Blue Lotus Ayurveda
Asheville, North Carolina
www.bluelotusayurveda.com

Embrace Ayurveda - Sarah Kruse
Seattle, Washington
www.embrace-ayurveda.com

Essential Oils

Floracopeia
www.floracopeia.com

Young Living
www.youngliving.com

doTerra
www.doterra.com

Neti Pots

Himalayan Chandra Neti Pots
www.Netipot.com

Enema Supplies

I love the **Aliva Medical Grade Silicone Enema Bag**

Also a **stainless steel bucket system** is good, cleanable, and reusable.

Blonde or Gold Roast Organic Coffee
www.sawilsons.com

Panchakarma Retreats

Shakti Veda Collective

A collective of Ayurvedic practitioners and massage therapists who co-operate to offer you a most beautiful panchakarma experience on Kauai.

Your Panchakarma Retreat Includes:

- An in-depth consultation to determine your optimum panchakarma therapies, foods, and practices.
- Thorough instructions for a 5-6 day home preparation.
- 5-7 Days of intensive treatments with us.
- A treatment day consists of approximately 3 hours of warm oil massage, aromatic steam, and adjunct bliss therapies chosen to bring balance to you specifically.
- All herbal preparations during your panchakarma.
- All organic, fresh food from our farm, ayurvedically chosen to bring about a gentle cleansing and a resetting of your digestive system.
- Emotional release strategies as appropriate.
- Instruction in yoga asana, meditation, and pranayam as appropriate.
- Sound healing
- Aromatherapy
- A full and detailed program of rasayana practices following panchakarma.
- Guidance and instruction for a follow up program to support your body, mind, emotions, and life at a new level of health, clarity, vitality, and peace within.

Made in the USA
Coppell, TX
01 March 2020

16406173R00108